FOKKER F27/FAIRCHILD F27/ FOKKER F50

First published in the UK in 1995 by
Airlife Publishing Ltd

British Library Cataloguing in Publication Data
A catalogue record for this book is available from the British Library

ISBN 1 85310 520 1

Typeset by Litho Link Ltd, Welshpool, Powys, Wales
Printed in Hong Kong

Airlife Publishing Ltd

101 Longden Road, Shrewsbury SY3 9EB

Introduction

When captain Hugo V.B. Burgerhout taxied Fokker F27 prototype PH-NIV out to the runway, after the plane had left Hangar 9 of Fokker Aircraft B.V. at Amsterdam's Schiphol Airport, on 24 November 1955, no-one could have known that one of the world's most successful commuter aircraft, which has been operated by over 220 airlines so far, was waiting for its maiden flight. Yet, launching a product of this size had been a major problem for Fokker, because, following World War II, facilities at Amsterdam Airport lay in destruction and the traditional aircraft manufacturer had tried to keep its divisions alive by constructing gliders and one-engined trainers. Additionally, military C-47s were converted or reconverted into DC-3s for civil transport use. This business led Fokker to think about possible markets for a plane replacing the old DC-3. Market analysis yielded a perspective of the airlines' prerequisites for such an aircraft and led directly to the outline and design of the Fokker F27 'Friendship'. In 1950 Fokker's chief-designer H.C. van Meerten introduced a twin-engined plane for up to thirty-two passengers, known as 'Project P.275', the actual F27 predecessor. The Dutch Institute for Aircraft Development (NIV) provided financial support for the production of four prototypes and Fokker registered its first prototype 'PH-NIV' to symbolically acknowledge this backing.

And here we are back, remembering the memorable day in autumn 1955, when Hugo Burgerhout — the plane's engines roaring — released the brakes to take-off for the F27's 34-minutes' maiden flight. Remarkable advantages over the aircraft's competitors were the turboprop-engine equipment, at a time when piston-engines were still common, and the incorporation of a pressurized cabin, allowing extended service ceilings. The plane's high-wing arrangement was epoch-making and later on was adopted by various other aircraft manufacturers, like Aérospaciale (ATR), Dornier (Do 228/328) or de Havilland Canada (DHC 6/7/8).

Loading, unloading and embarkation were facilitated and the plane's lift characteristics could be improved. A disadvantage, however, proved to be the poor absorption of kinetic energy released when crash-landing. During manufacture, high pressure and temperature method of joining metal sections together was firstly used. Despite the plane's advantages, sales-figures increased slowly in the beginning. This changed after advertising and marketing had been intensified by Fokker's sales director F.J.L. Diepen, who launched the 'Customer Training Centre' in 1958, training crews of F27 customers. Six basic Fokker F27 versions were offered, but a great variety of modified models evolved during

TABLE OF COMPARISONS						
FOKKER						
Version:	F27-100	F27-200	F27-300	F27-400	F27-500	F27-600	F50 (F27-050)
First flight date:	29 Jan. 1957	20 Sept. 1959	1 May 1960	6 Oct. 1961	15 Nov. 1967	28 Nov. 1968	28 Dec. 1985
Max. accommodation:	52	52	52	52	56	52	60
Wing span (m / ft):	29.00 / 95.2	29.00 / 95.2	29.00 / 95.2	29.00 / 95.2	29.00 / 95.2	29.00 / 95.2	29.00 / 95.2
Length (m / ft):	23.56 / 77.3	23.56 / 77.3	23.56 / 77.3	23.56 / 77.3	25.06 / 82.3	23.56 / 77.3	25.19 / 82.6
Height (m / ft):	8.50 / 27.11	8.50 / 27.11	8.50 / 27.11	8.50 / 27.11	8.71 / 28.7	8.50 / 27.11	8.60 / 28.2
Max. t / o weight (kg / lb):	18,370 / 40,500	19,730 / 43,500	18,370 / 40,500	19,730 / 43,500	20,410 / 45,000	20,410 / 45,000	20,820 / 45,900
Operating weight (kg / lb):	10,295 / 22,696	10,525 / 23,404	9,973 / 21,987	10,203 / 22,495	11,950 / 26,345	11,314 / 24,943	12,383 / 27,300
Max. cruise speed (kmh / kt):	428 / 231	474 / 256	428 / 231	474 / 256	480 / 259	480 / 259	532 / 287
Max. range (km / nm):	2,020 / 1,091	2,070 / 1,116	2,020 / 1,091	2,070 / 1,116	1,742 / 935	1,926 / 1,020	2,797 / 1,510
Service ceiling (m / ft):	9,020 / 29,600	9,140 / 30,000	9,020 / 29,600	8,890 / 29,500	8,890 / 29,500	8,890 / 29,500	7,620 / 25,000
Max. fuel capacity (kg / lb):	4,109 / 9,059	4,109 / 9,059	4,109 / 9,059	4,109 / 9,059	4,109 / 9,059	4,109 / 9,059	4,123 / 9,090
Engine equipment: 2	R-R Dart 7 514-7	R-R Dart 7 532-7R	R-R Dart 7 514-7	R-R Dart 7 532-7R	R-R Dart 536-7R	R-R Dart 536-7R	2 PWC PW 124
Numbers produced:	85	115	13	127	124	95	197 (to March 1994)

FAIRCHILD					
Version:	F-27	F-27A	F-27F	F-27J / M	FH-227
First flight date:	12 April 1958	1958	Jan. 1960	1964	2 Feb. 1966
Max. accommodation:	44	44	44	48	56
Wing span (m / ft):	29.00 / 95.2	29.00 / 95.2	29.00 / 95.2	29.00 / 95.2	29.00 / 95.2
Length (m / ft):	23.53 / 77.2	23.53 / 77.2	23.53 / 77.2	23.53 / 77.2	25.48 / 82.8
Height (m / ft):	8.40 / 27.6	8.40 / 27.6	8.40 / 27.6	8.40 / 27.6	8.41 / 27.5
Max. t / o weight (kg / lb):	17,870 / 39,400	19,050 / 42,000	19,050 / 42,000	19,050 / 42,000	19,730 / 43,500
Operating weight (kg / lb):	9,373 / 20,664	9,685 / 21,353	9,685 / 21,353	9,707 / 21,353	10,313 / 22,736
Max. cruise speed (kmh / kt):	439 / 237	483 / 261	483 / 261	478 / 258	473 / 255
Max. range (km / nm):	2,906 / 1,569	2,930 / 1,582	4,540 / 2,451	4,500 / 2,433	4,315 / 2329
Service ceiling (m / ft):	9,020 / 29,600	9,935 / 32,600	10,120 / 33,200	9,935 / 32,600	8,535 / 28,000
Max. fuel capacity (kg / lb):	4,046 / 8,920	4,046 / 8,920	4,046 / 8,920	4,046 / 8,920	4,046 / 8,920
Engine equipment: 2	R-R Dart 6 511	R-R Dart 6 514-7	R-R Dart 6 529-7	R-R Dart 6 532-7	R-R Dart 10 542-7
Numbers produced:	48	44 + 3 F-27B	18	14 / 2	78

the thirty years of serial production.

Compared to the prototype, F27-100 was increased in length by equipping the nose with a weather radar system that became embodied in all further series. The first F27-100 was finally delivered to Aer Lingus in late 1958. F27-200 is characterized by more powerful engines and a stronger landing gear. Additional bag-tanks and reduced minimum runway length in landing were this model's outstanding innovations. F27-300 'Combiplane' had an additional side cargo door for use as combined passenger/cargo aircraft. Only thirteen units, however, were produced. F27-400 was developed from F27-200 version and made its maiden flight in late 1961. This version could also be modified for military or rescue purposes (F27-400M). In late 1967 an elongated version was presented, sold as F27-500.

An interesting special modification of the F27-500 model is the F27-500RF. The acronym stands for 'rough field' and indicates these planes being equipped with a reinforced landing gear for operations on non-tarred runways. F27-600, finally, is similar to the Mk 200 model, but a side cargo door is installed and the cabin floor is not reinforced. To gain foothold in the North American market, Fokker decided to authorize Fairchild Engine and Airplane Corporation to produce the Fokker F27 under licence. After the ATC certification had been issued in October 1957, Fairchild started its production at Hagerstown/Maryland. Many secondary systems for the aircraft were now provided by U.S. firms and European standards were modified to fit the needs of the U.S. market. Despite some minor differences, the first version, called F-27, is similar to the Fokker F27-100, and F-27A matches F27-200. F-27B, of which only three units have been built, is equipped with a large cargo door. F-27E is an elongated version for 52 passengers and is 1.49 metres longer than the standard models. F-27F was especially designed for business use and can be operated on runways with a minimum length of 1130 metres when fully loaded. The last F-27 models J and M are equipped with more powerful engines, with F-27M being a modification for use on high-altitude airports in South America and therefore fitted out with a larger propeller. When the Fairchild and Hiller Company merged in September 1964, an elongated F-27 model was developed and sold under the renamed title 'FH-227'. This aircraft has been produced in various series, named FH-227/B/C/D/E, with only minor modifications.

When the licensing agreement came to an end in December 1968, Fairchild-Hiller's FH-227 production finished after the delivery of the 206th aircraft. Fokker's F27 was produced until spring 1987, when the 786th (including F-27/FH-227) and last Fokker F27-500 was delivered to Air Winconsin. This was, however, far away from being the end of the F27 conception. In 1983 Fokker announced the development of the Fokker F50 under the names 'Project P.335' and Fokker F27-050. The roll-out of the first prototype of the F-27-successor was on 28 December 1985. F27 and F50 look very similar at first glance, but nearly 80 per cent of the parts used in the F50 are completely new. Visible innovations include the smaller and more rectangular-shaped cabin windows, whose number is doubled, and a larger front door. The power units cannot be compared with the Fokker F27's engines. Fokker employs Pratt & Whitney Canada PW 124 turboprops and consequently the engine nacelles had to be fundamentally altered. The plane is enlarged by 1.63 metres against the Fokker F27 standard model and is designed for 50–60 passengers. Launch customers were Ansett Australia, DLT, Maersk Air and Austrian Airlines. In the beginning Fokker experienced considerable delays in delivering the ordered aircraft, because with the F50 and F100, two new planes had been developed simultaneously. But today, serial production runs as planned and it seems as if the Fokker F50 could be as successful as the 'Friendship' has been.

AER LINGUS (EI/EIN)   Ireland

The Republic of Ireland's national flag-carrier Aer Lingus was founded in 1936 and began operating on 27 May that year, with a sole five-seat de Havilland Dragon Rapid flying from Dublin to Bristol under the name 'Aer Lingus Teoranta'. Until the end of 1937 the network included London, Isle of Man, and Liverpool. During World War II most services had to be suspended except for the Dublin-Liverpool flight which was maintained with a Douglas DC-3. Merger with Aerlinte Eireann Teoranta in 1947 created the airline's current name 'Aer Lingus'. Flights to British and European destinations, like Paris and Amsterdam, were taken up again. The airline had to wait for over ten years before transatlantic flights were permitted by the Irish government, but in late 1958 a Lockheed Super Constellation operated from Dublin via Shannon to Boston and New York, a routing which still appears in Aer Lingus' schedule. Two years after the initial flight, the Constellations were already replaced by Boeing B-707s and in 1971 Boeing B-747s took over the route. Aer Lingus holds interests in many hotels, catering and computer services and other airlines, including a 100 per cent share in Irish Helicopters Ltd, 75 per cent in Aer Turas and a minority holding in Air Tara/Guinness Peat Aviation. Aer Lingus Commuter was founded in 1984 as a subsidiary, providing services on domestic and minor international Aer Lingus routes. In September 1988 the airline decided to order Fokker F50s for these services. Six units of that type and four Saab SF340s replaced Aer Lingus Commuter's Shorts SH360s. Just having completed flight EI266 from Dublin, Fokker F50, EI-FKF *St. Ultan*, is here seen rolling-in at Birmingham on 25 September 1992. Fokker F50 flights cover routes from Dublin to Birmingham, Bristol, Brussels, Cork, Edinburgh, Glasgow, Manchester, and Shannon. They sport the airline's traditional bold green livery and the white shamrock tail logo. The green roof is separated from a dark green windowline by a band of bright blue, with the lower section in white and the underside in grey. In January 1994, the company ordered three A330s which were leased from ILFC in May 1994 and will replace the old Boeing B-747-100s. Further long-term plans include the substitution of most of the Boeing B-737s by Airbus A319/320/321s. Aer Lingus' ICAO call sign is 'SHAMROCK'. *(W. Kathe)*

AEROCARIBE (QA/CBE)   Mexico

Aerocaribe was founded in 1974 under the name 'Aerovias Caribe' at Cancun and operated charter flights with Convair CV340s and CV440s. In the early 1980s a Convair CV240 and an Embraer 110 Bandeirante joined the fleet and in 1987 a second Metropolitan flew for Aerocaribe. The company operates scheduled passenger flights between commercial and resort centres on the Yucatan Peninsula, throughout the states of Yucatan and Quintana Roo. Main routes are Cancun-Cozumel, Cancun-Cozumel-Chichen Itza and Cancun-Merida. Additionally, charter flight activities from Cancun to various places are carried out. In the late 1980s Aerocaribe began modernizing its fleet and withdrawing the old Convairs. The first Fairchild F-27, XA-MCJ, was taken into service in late 1987. Two additional ex-Britt Air Fairchild F-27s joined the fleet in February 1990. In November 1990 Aerocaribe became a subsidiary of Mexicana. Although earlier plans included the fusion of Aerocaribe and Aerocozumel, both airlines were still operated separately thereafter. In December 1993 the regional subsidiary of Mexicana got two Douglas DC-9s. The jets replaced the Fairchild F-27s on some routes from Merida and Cancun which are run in competition with Aviacsa's Fokker F100. Today a fleet of four Fairchild F-27J/Fs, four FH-227B/C/Ds and two DC-9s is maintained. The aircraft are operated for Mexicana providing feeder connections to Mexicana's major hubs, using MX flight numbers. If required, Fairchilds can be interchanged with the affiliated carriers Aerocozumel and Aero-monterrey. Seen here at Miami International Airport on 5 October 1988, Fairchild F-27F, N27GC, is depicted. This aircraft is one of the older F-27s, which was delivered to General Tire & Rubber Company in 1958 and later on converted into F-series. It did not operate with Aerocaribe for very long. The airline's ICAO call sign is 'AEROCARIBE'. *(W. Kathe)*

AEROLINEAS URUGUAYAS (AUY)   Uruguay

In March 1990 the company was founded as a cargo operator which succeeded the former Aero Uruguay. The company's home bases are Montevideo-Carrasco and Colonia. Aerolineas Uruguayas operates one Boeing B-707/331C on cargo flights to Miami and some places in South America and a couple of Fairchild F-27s. The first one came from the bankrupt's estate of Aero Uruguay and continued the scheduled operations from Colonia-Laguna de los Patos to Buenos Aires which had been suspended in January 1990. The following year a Fokker F27 was leased from Fuerza Aerea Argentina for some time, until Aerolineas Uruguayas purchased two more Fairchild FH-227s from Delta Air Transport/Belgium in May 1992. The full livery applied to the Boeing B-707 consists of three diagonal stripes half way between cockpit and wing in blue, yellow and red with a gap between the latter two. Within the broader blue stripe, 'Cargo' titles are applied. This arrangement is repeated beneath the tail, the rest of the fuselage remains white, with 'Aerolineas Uruguayas' titles in the middle. The colourful tail displays an oblique white 'U' on a blue and red field surrounded by a thin yellow line. The remaining parts of the tail are coloured in deep blue. Seen here in summer 1993, the Fairchild FH-227B CX-BQU is shown. This plane had operated for Delta Air Transport, before, registered OO-DTA. It has a one-class 48-seat configuration and a slightly modified colour scheme: the stripes on the front fuselage are applied as described, but not repeated below the tail. The fin is coloured in solid blue, similar to KLM Cityhopper. The airline's ICAO call sign is 'AUSA'. *(Author's Collection)*

AIR ALGERIE (AH/DAH)

Algeria

The roots of Air Algerie trace back to the year 1946, when the airline was founded by some French-Algerian businessmen under the name 'Compagnie Générale de Transports Aériens' (C.G.T.A). In the early days only charter flights were operated. In 1953 C.G.T.A merged with its main competitor Cie. Air Transport and the new name 'Air Algerie' was created. At that time a fleet of three Douglas DC-3s, ten DC-4s and three Nord 2501 Nordatlases was maintained; two Lockheed L-749 Constellations were taken over a short time afterwards. One year later the first domestic service started on the Algiers-Ghardaia-Golea route. In 1959 Air Algerie's first jet, a Caravelle 3, joined the fleet. After seven years of war, Algeria gained independence from France in July 1962; months of negotiations followed and finally the state acquired a fifty-one per cent shareholding in Air Algerie on 18 February 1963. Ten years later the airline became entirely state-controlled. In 1968 the old Douglas fleet was replaced by four ex-Lufthansa Convair CV640s on domestic routes. In the same year, the 'Société de Travail Aérien'

was founded as an air-taxi company, taken over by Air Algerie in 1972, then transformed into a domestic airline and finally integrated into Air Algerie in 1989. In 1971/72 the first Boeing B-727-200 and B-737-200 jets were delivered which gradually superseded the Caravelles. For domestic services five Nord 262s were purchased. Until today nearly 50 per cent of Air Algerie's flights are domestic. Nevertheless, the European network was expanded during the late 1970s. Additionally Air Algerie has developed to be one of the main carriers of 'hadj'-flights to Mecca (Jeddah). Today the airline operates a fleet of sixteen Boeing B-737-200s, eleven Boeing B-727-200s, four Airbus A310s, three Boeing B-767s, two Lockheed 382 Hercules freighters and seven Fokker F27s for the minor domestic routes. A Fokker F27-400M, 7T-VRR, is seen here at Palma de Mallorca in April 1993, on flight AH2000 from Algiers. It should be noted that Palma is the only international destination that is regularly served by a Fokker F27 twice a week. The airline's ICAO call sign is 'AIR ALGERIE'. *(Author's Collection)*

AIR CORTEZ (AB/AJY)   United States of America

Air Cortez was founded in 1976 under the name 'Schlick Air Service dba'. On 1 January 1977 the airline started regular services from its home base at Ontario Airport in California. Flight operations began with a fleet of Cessna 414 Chancellor and Beechcraft G-18 / C-45H propliners. Air Cortez operated international scheduled flights from Ontario and San Diego to Guaymas, Mulege and Loreto in Mexico and regular domestic flights in California, Nevada and Arizona. The privately-owned airline also had charter contracts for services within the Southern states of the USA, and to Mexico. In the early 1980s Air Cortez bought three Fairchild Ind. F-27Js for the main routes and the name was changed to 'Air Cortez International'. The airline's regular livery consisted of four stripes in red, orange and yellow along the windowline, tapering towards the front and the tail. The logo shining on the tail-fin was a stylized 'a' in the same four

colours. In 1984, the international services were suspended and the main scheduled service still operated was linking Las Vegas and Grand Canyon Airport several times a day with Cessna 402 and Fairchild F-27 aircraft. In May 1987 the airline had to suspend operations entirely and went bankrupt. At that time the fleet consisted of two Cessna 402s that had replaced the Cessna 414, two Beech 18s and five Fairchild F-27s. The Fairchild F-27J N311NA had only operated for a very short period and still had basic Swed-Air colours. Two other F-27s were sold to Toucan Air/Ontario, but one of them was scrapped immediately. The two remaining Fairchild F-27s were stored at Las Vegas. Taken in December 1983 is ground photo of the Fairchild Ind. F-27J N712AB, built in 1962.
(Author's Collection)

AIR JET (YH/AIJ)   France

Air Jet was founded as 'Compagnie Air Jet' in 1980 and began charter flights in the same year with Beechcraft King Air F90s and one Fokker F27-600 which was bought from Iberia. In 1984 the company bought a second F27 and began operating scheduled domestic passenger flights with charter operations throughout Europe and the Mediterranean. Daily services linked Lyon with Avignon. The airline is privately-owned and a division of Jet Services Group, a forwarding agency with its main activities in France and Belgium. In May 1987 a third Fokker F27 was purchased from Rio Sul (Brazil). This aircraft was used on cargo flights from Orly to Bordeaux for Jet Services carrying 'Jet Services' titles. At the same time plans to buy a plane with a 10-15 tonnes cargo capacity were elaborated. In autumn 1989, Jet Services introduced their new colour scheme on the Fokker F27 F-GHRC (ex Sudan Airways ST-ALF) for the first time. In 1990 an all-Fokker F27 fleet of five units

was maintained. They are all equipped with a 48-seat one-class configuration but are quickly convertible to freighters, and fly on regular cargo services from Paris-Orly to Avignon, Agen and Nancy and on passenger flights between Lyon and Avignon. The first BAe 146 was delivered in October 1991 for the daily night post service from Paris-Orly to Avignon. In November 1993 the airline leased a BAe 146-300QC from Mid Pacific (USA) until an own BAe 146-300QC was delivered in early 1994.
Here you see the airline's oldest Fokker F27-600, F-GCJV, at Avignon Airport on 31 May 1986, in Air Jet's old colour scheme. The tail fin displayed two broad green beams with the company's logo, the head and the wing of a flying horse, in between. A broad, bright green cheatline ran at window level. It should be noted that, today this aircraft is still in service. Air Jet's ICAO call sign is 'AIR JET'.
(W. Kathe)

AIRLIFT (RD/AIR)

United States of America

The airline was formed under the name 'Riddle Aviation Company' on 25 May 1945. After a first change of this name into 'Riddle Airlines' in 1952, the final title 'Airlift International' was adopted in March 1964. Four years later, Slick Airways was purchased by Airlift and integrated. The airline concentrated on passenger and cargo charter flights throughout the USA and abroad with Douglas DC-8 equipment. Mainly places in the Caribbean and in South America were served. In June 1981 Airlift had to suspend operations and filed for bankruptcy for the first time. Operations, however, could be resumed with two DC-8-50s and one DC-8-61 in 1982. On 31 December 1985 operations had to be stopped again, but the airline reorganised and began new flight activities the following year, this time with one DC-8-54 and one Fairchild FH-227C. In January 1988 the airline could sell its last two DC-8-61s that had been inactive for some time, to Airborne Express, after being hush-kitted at Orlando. In August 1988 Airlift added two more ex-Swed-Air Fairchild F-27s to the fleet and introduced a new livery. Some

more Fairchild F-27s were taken over from Horizon Air in late 1988. They mainly operated on flights from Fort Lauderdale to the Bahamas. Some F-27s therefore carried additional 'Lacayan Beach Casino Express' titles. In early 1989 three Fairchild F-27s were leased to the Mexican carrier Aerovias Oaxaquenas. In 1990 and early 1991 Airlift had to face heavy financial troubles again and made a high loss. In June 1991 the company had to suspend operations for the third time and was liquidated one month later. The planes were stored at Miami for over a year before they could be sold to Islena, Honduras. The photo shows the airline's first Fairchild FH-227C, N374RD, seen here at Miami International Airport in October 1988. The aircraft displays Airlift's last livery with its seven narrow green and brown windowlines underlining green 'Airlift' titles and tail half in white, half in green. This plane is the fourth oldest of the FH-227 serial production and had originally been delivered to Mohawk Airlines in 1966. Airlift's ICAO call sign was 'AIRLIFT'. *(W. Kathe)*

AIRLINES OF SOUTH AUSTRALIA (GJ/AOS)

Australia

Airlines of South Australia (ASA) was formed on 4 November 1927 as 'Guinea Airways'. It firstly linked Lae to the mining centre Wau in New Guinea. Australian services started in February 1937 with scheduled flights between Adelaide and Darwin. In July 1959 the Ansett Airline Group took over Guinea Airways and renamed it 'Ansett Airlines of South Australia' in January 1960. Its maintenance and operational base has been at Adelaide ever since. After July 1981, when Ansett had given more independence to its subsidiaries, the airline was just called Airlines of South Australia. Its colourful livery displayed basic white colours, with a triple cheatline. A yellow line ran along the windows, with a black stripe below and a red above. The cheatline was interrupted beneath the cockpit to give room to similarly triple-coloured 'ASA' titles. 'Airlines of South Australia' titles were applied above. The cheatline was extended curving onto the fin, where it ended as a stylized bird by three black crossing lines forming the wings, tail and head. A fleet of four Fokker F27 turbo-props operated daily or weekday flights between Adelaide and Ceduna, Kingscote/Kangaroo Island, Mt. Gambier, Port Lincoln and Whyalla in South Australia and to Broken Hill in New South Wales. Services to Streaky Bay were offered in association with Rossair. Although the airline was an Ansett subsidiary, it had to suspend operations by the end of June 1986, because the company's losses and debits became extremely high and the routes more and more unprofitable. In July 1986, Kendell Airlines, operating a fleet of Swearingen Metro IIs and Saab SF340s, took over all the routes of former Airlines of South Australia, except for the Adelaide-Kingscote service. The aircraft were integrated into Ansett Australia. The photo shows VH-FNR, on the ramp at Adelaide in April 1985. It has been the airline's only Fokker F27-600, with its 40-seat configuration. All the other F27s were Mk 200s with 44 seats. The aircraft had been delivered to Ansett in 1967 as a F27-400 and was converted in the late 1970s. In November 1991 Ansett sold the aircraft to Morning-star Air Express, Canada, where it operates for Federal Express, registered C-GBWC, on parcel flights. (Author's Collection)

AIR NEW ZEALAND (NZ/ANZ)   New Zealand

Air New Zealand traces its roots back to the formation of Tasman Empire Airways Ltd. (TEAL), a British-Australian-New Zealand joint venture, in 1939. The Auckland-Sydney route was initially served on 30 April 1940, with a 19-seat S.30 Empire amphibian. Various flying-boat models were operated, until the Douglas DC-6 replaced the amphibians in 1954. One year before, Australia had acquired the British share in the airline and in 1961 New Zealand gained full ownership. In 1965 the company was renamed 'Air New Zealand' and three Douglas DC-8s were the airline's first jets, followed by DC-10s in 1973. On 1 April 1978, the modern Air New Zealand was formed by the merger of Air New Zealand and the domestic carrier New Zealand National Airways Corporation (NAL). The latter had been founded in 1947 serving several domestic routes and using S25 Sunderland flying-boats. During the 1950s and 1960s the airline's domestic network was served with a Douglas DC-3, Vickers Viscount and Fokker F27 fleet, before the Boeing B-737-200 was added in 1968. Today, the United Air New Zealand holds interests in Cook Island Airways, Polynesian Airlines, Mount Cook Airline and Air Pacific. A fleet of Boeing B-737-200/300s, Boeing B-767-200/300s and Boeing B-747-200/400 series is maintained. The airline offers scheduled services to about 30 domestic destinations (including NZ Airlink), fourteen places in Australia/Oceania and on fifteen inter-continental routes. European destinations are Frankfurt and London. In the early 1990s domestic operations were reorganized: the company's Fokker F27s were gradually withdrawn from use after August 1990, and main domestic airports, like Hamilton, Invercargill, Napier and Palmerston North were expanded for Boeing B-737 operations. Air Nelson, a private airline based at Nelson, was renamed Air New Zealand Link after its association with Air New Zealand. It established a commuter system providing feeder connections to Air New Zealand's major hubs. The aircraft (Swearingen Metros and Saab SF 340s) are operated in Air New Zealand colours using NZ flight numbers. In early 1989 Air New Zealand was privatised. Minority shareholders are Qantas, Japan Air Lines and American Airlines; the majority was taken over by Brierley Investments, partly passed on to the airline's employees and to the public. In early 1994 Air New Zealand extended its Boeing B-737-200 fleet by six ex-Britannia aircraft. All B-737-200s are now equipped with Nordam hush-kits. Here you see Fokker F27-100, ZK-BXG, which had been delivered to NAL in 1961. It sports the airline's traditional livery, a blue and turquoise twin cheatline and a white tail logo representing a traditional Maori symbol. Air New Zealand's ICAO call sign is 'NEW ZEALAND'. *(Author's Collection)*

AIR N.S.W. (WX/NSW)
Australia

Air N.S.W., or giving in its full title, 'Air New South Wales', has been one of the most traditional Australian regional carriers. The airline was originally founded in 1934 under the name 'Butler Air Transport'. In 1958 it became part of the Ansett Airline Group and was run as 'Ansett Airlines of New South Wales' until July 1981. At that time a fleet of six Fokker F27-500s was maintained. Until 1988 the airline's official name was 'Air New South Wales'; after that year, it was called 'Air N.S.W.'. In early 1990 the company was renamed 'Ansett N.S.W.' again, and today it has completely been amalgamated and runs under the simple name 'Ansett Express'. The aircraft sport full Ansett livery. After the delivery of Fokker F50s in 1987, the F27s gradually left the fleet. Fokker F27-500F VH-FCD was sold to Ladeco Chile in January 1988, another F27 was leased to the same company. In February 1989 two Fokker F27s were sold to Mesaba Airlines, a Northwest Airlink company, and the last F27 was withdrawn from use in late 1989. Today a fleet of five Fokker F50s and

eight Fokker F28s, six of them taken over from East West Airlines, is maintained. In January 1993 two BAe 146-300s joined the fleet of 'Ansett Express'. The airline's operational base is still Sydney's Kingsford Smith Airport. Scheduled passenger services are provided to about thirty places all over New South Wales, Tasmania, Queensland and Norfolk Island. Major routes include Sydney-Devonport, Brisbane-Norfolk Island, Sydney-Griffith-Narrandera and Newcastle-Coolangatta-Brisbane. A lot of these services are feeder operations for Ansett. Depicted here in late 1987, is Fokker F27-500F, VH-FCC, displaying full Ansett Australia 'flying stars' tail colours, a plain white fuselage and large 'Air N.S.W.' titles behind the cockpit. The aircraft had been directly delivered to Ansett in 1976. In February 1989 it was sold to Mesaba Airlines, registered N282MA, and today still operates for Northwest Airlink. Air N.S.W.'s ICAO call sign has been 'NEWSOUTH'. *(Author's Collection)*

AIR SINAI (DP/ASD)   Egypt

The history of Air Sinai dates back to April 1982, the time when Israel returned the Sinai to Egypt, which explains the airline's name. It succeeded the former Nefertiti Aviation operating on the Cairo-Tel Aviv route. Air Sinai is a regional airline associated with Egypt Air and operating on less frequent domestic routes for Egypt Air with two Fokker F27s and a temporarily leased Boeing B-737-200 (each in full Air Sinai colours). The Boeing B-737 is also used on the Cairo-Tel Aviv service and the Fokker F27 on the second international flight from Sharm-el-Sheik to Eilat. The Fokker F27s belong to the 500 series and have a one-class 52-seat configuration. In the mid 1980s a Boeing B-707 was leased from Egypt Air and operated for Air Sinai on domestic scheduled and international charter flights for a short period. In February 1987 the Israeli charter and domestic airline Arkia got permission to operate joint charter services together with Air Sinai from Eilat to Luxor (primarily one-day trips) with DHC 7 or Boeing B-707. Due to the reduction of political tensions between Israel and Egypt, more flights between the two countries were possible and so Air Sinai began a pool operation with Arkia from Sharm-el-Sheik to Tel Aviv in March 1993. Today, the company's two Fokker F27s are mostly used on scheduled domestic flights for Egypt Air from Luxor and Cairo to various places in the Nile Valley. These routes include services between Cairo and Alexandria and between Luxor and Abu Simbel. The Boeing B-737-200 operates between Luxor and Aswan, on scheduled flights from Cairo and on charter services to Europe on behalf of Egypt Air. The company plans to replace the Fokker F27s by Canadair Regional Jets RJ 100s. A yellow cheatline and a thinner black stripe below the window-line characterizes the livery of the fuselage, on the tail-fin shines the airline's logo: a blue circle with a blue bottom — symbolizing the sea — with the Air Sinai script in it, a yellow line standing for the desert, with stylized palm trees and an aircraft between the trees.

SU-GAE, one of the company's Fokker F27s, is here depicted at Munich-Riem Airport on 29 March 1989, whilst stopping on its flight to Fokker for maintenance. On the back cover SU-GAF, one of the company's Fokker F27s, is seen on the tarmac of Munich Airport on 28 August 1989, during a fuel-stop on its ferry flight to Fokker. Air Sinai's international call sign is 'AIR SINAI'. *(W. Kathe)*

AIR TANZANIA (TC/ATC)   Tanzania

After the collapse of East African Airways (EAA), a joint venture airline of Tanzania, Kenya and Uganda, the three East African states each formed their own national carrier. EAA had suspended operations on 28 February 1977, and as it was difficult to establish a national airline immediately, the Tanzanian president Nyerere asked Mozambique Airlines (DETA) for help. One Boeing B-737 and one Fokker F27 were taken over on short-term lease. Two more Fokker F27s came from the bankrupt's estate of the former EAA. The first points served were Lusaka (Zambia), Maputo (Mozambique) and several places in Tanzania. On 1 June 1977, Air Tanzania was officially founded and the network was expanded to eleven domestic and six international destinations. The Boeing B-737 fleet grew to four units until 1979 and four DHC 6 Twin Otters linked minor domestic places. In 1980 two efforts were made to start long-haul flights. A Boeing B-720 only operated for two months and an old TWA Boeing B-707 for half a year on services to London and Zürich. Both efforts failed, however, and these operations had to be suspended in November 1980. In 1982 Air Tanzania founded two subsidiaries, Air Catering Ltd at Dar-es-Salaam and DAHACO (Dar-es-Salaam Handling Company), with the help of East African Development Bank, SAS and the ministries of development of the Scandinavian states. Air Tanzania's current fleet consists of three DHC 6 Twin Otter, three Fokker F27s and two Boeing B737s. These planes serve 20 domestic and 12 international destinations; Nairobi, Djibouti, Jeddah, Muscat, Maputo, Lilongwe, Dubai, Entebbe, Harare, Lusaka, Bujumbura and Kigali. After ten years Air Tanzania started European services again in June 1991. On the weekly flights Dar-es-Salaam-Frankfurt and Dar-es-Salaam-Milan-London an Ethiopian Boeing B-767-200 in full Air Tanzania colours was used. This service ceased in March 1992 and the Boeing B-767 was returned to Ethiopian Airways again. In autumn 1993 Air Tanzania leased out a Fokker F27 to Air Star Zanzibar for regional services from Zanzibar to places in Kenya and Tanzania. Depicted here on an exceptional stop at Munich on 10 April 1988 on its way to the Netherlands (for overhaul), you see Fokker F27-600 (CRF), 5H-MPU. The airline's international ICAO call sign is 'TANZANIA'. *(W. Kathe)*

AIR UK (UK/UKA)
United Kingdom

Air UK was formed in January 1980 by the merger of four airlines: Air Anglia, Air Wales, Air Westward and British Island Airways. Air Anglia had been founded ten years before and had developed a solid network in England's southeast and Scotland; Air Wales had only existed for three years flying from its base at Cardiff to England, the Channel Islands, Belgium and France. Air Westward undertook scheduled operations out of Exeter to various places on the continent, and British Island Airways, ex-British United, linked the British mainland with Northern Ireland, the Isle of Man and the Channel Islands. Air UK started with a fleet of Embraer 110 Bandeirantes, Fokker F27s, F28s, Handley Page Heralds and BAC 1/11s. In 1982 the passenger tour charter operations — including BAC 1/11 equipment — were sold to the 'new' British Island Air. In June 1987 Air UK ordered two Boeing B-737-400s for its new subsidiary Air UK Leisure which was founded at the same time. The home base of the new airline was Stansted. Thirty per cent is held by Air UK, 30 per cent by B&C Holding and 40 per cent by the travel agency Viking International. The airline began operating in spring 1988 using two Boeing B-737-200s. Recently, Leisure International Airways (LIA) has been founded offering long-haul charter flights with Boeing B-767-300s. With the delivery of the second BAe 146 in late 1988, a new colour scheme replaced the all-blue livery: a white fuselage with three cheatlines in different blue tones that taper off on the tail and pass into a fluttering Union Jack. In June 1992 the first Fokker 100s were taken in service on some major European routes. Today, Air UK operates a fleet of fourteen Fokker F27-100/200/500/600s, ten BAe 146s (all versions), one Shorts SD360 and nine Fokker F100s. Air UK is Britain's third largest scheduled airline with over 1200 flights weekly. It is fully owned by Air UK Group Ltd., a holding with British Air Transport Ltd (85.1 per cent) and KLM Royal Dutch Airlines (14.9 per cent) sharing interests. Fifteen domestic locations are served from the main hubs at London-Stansted, Norwich, Edinburgh and Aberdeen and international destinations include the central hub at Amsterdam and Bergen, Stavanger, Düsseldorf, Frankfurt, Brussels, Paris, Nice and Florence.

Fokker F27-200, G-BDVS, is here seen at Amsterdam-Schiphol before taking off on Air UK flight UK783 to Teeside, on 1 August 1992. The aircraft had been delivered to Malayan Airways in 1963 and later operated for Bangladesh Biman. *(W. Kathe)*

On the front cover: Fokker F27-200, G-BDVS, is seen while approaching London Heathrow Airport on 28 September 1992, coming in on flight UK228 from Guernsey. Air UK's ICAO call sign is 'UKAY'. *(W. Kathe)*

AIR WISCONSIN (ZW/AWI)   United States of America

Air Wisconsin was formed in 1963 at Appleton/Wisconsin and began flight operations between Appleton and Chicago on 23 August 1965. The privately-owned airline offered scheduled services in Wisconsin, Ohio and Illinois with a steadily growing fleet of Swearingen Metros and DHC7s. In 1983 Air Wisconsin became a subsidiary of the publicly-held Air Wis Services Inc., and served over twenty cities on regional flights throughout Connecticut, Illinois, Indiana, Michigan, Minnesota, Nebraska, Ohio and Wisconsin with BAC 1/11s and DHC7s. In summer 1983 the first BAe 146 joined the fleet, used on the route from Chicago to Fort Wayne, where the airline's maintenance base is located. In January 1985, Mississipi Valley Airlines became fully integrated after fusion of both airlines. So, Air Wisconsin had the first four Fokker F27s in its fleet, which was completed by another twelve F27s between September 1985 and June 1986. The Fokker F27-500 N513AW, delivered in June 1986, was the last Fokker F27 ever produced. In September 1986 Air Wisconsin ordered five BAe 146-300s, so the airline became launch customer for that elongated BAe 146-series. In the same year Air Wisconsin was bought by United Airlines

Corp. and integrated into United Express. Gradually the aircraft were painted up in United Express colours in 1987. In April 1991, Air Wisconsin bought Aspen Air (Denver), and intended to gain more independence from United Airlines that had little by little begun to operate the more profitable routes under its own flag and left the weaker services to Air Wisconsin and other airlines linked up as United Express. Aspen's routes to the skiing places in the Rockies and to California were kept alive, but the planes (Convair 580s and BAe 146s) were sold. In December 1990 Air Wisconsin ordered eight Dash 8s which were to replace the Fokker F27s in the long term. In January 1993 all the operations from Washington-Dulles were sold and the Dash 8s transferred to Atlantic Coast Airlines. The ATP services were sold to a new company named United Feeder Services and jet operations to CJT Holdings. The official new name is 'Air Wisconsin Airlines Corporation' (AWAC). Seen here in the airline's last colour scheme, Air Wisconsin's Fokker F27-500, N504AW, is depicted a few weeks after delivery in 1986. The airline's ICAO call sign is 'WISCONSIN'. *(Author's Collection)*

ALM-ANTILLEAN AIRLINES (LM/ALM)

Netherlands Antilles

ALM's history traces back to 1934, when KLM, the Dutch national airline, founded its Caribbean network. The official foundation of ALM-Antillean Airlines, however, was thirty years later, in August 1964, when KLM and the government of the Netherlands Antilles signed a contract to create ALM (Antilliaanse Luchtvaart Maatschappij). The flight activities started with three Convair CV340 piston-engined aircraft. In the late sixties ALM began operating scheduled international services to Miami (USA). In January 1969 the government of the Netherlands Antilles acquired 96 per cent of the airline, the other four per cent were still held by KLM. During the 1970s a McDonnell Douglas fleet of DC-6s, DC-8s and DC-9s was maintained. In June 1988 ALM bought two 50-seat Fairchild FH-227s from DAT-(Belgium) to operate flights linking Aruba, Bonaire and Curaçao and for routes to Venezuela. After two years they were

replaced by two ex-Presidential Dash 8-300s. The fleet of presently three MD-82s, two Dash DHC 8s and one Lockheed L-188 Electra is maintained at the airline's home base at Curaçao. The Lockheed Electra is a palletized freighter with a cargo capacity of 16 tonnes and operates scheduled freight services to Aruba, Bonaire, Haiti, Miami, Saint Maarten and Panama. The two Dash 8s are equipped with 50 seats and serve the local destinations and Barquisimeto, Valencia, Caracas and Puerto la Cruz in Venezuela. The MD-82s are used for major regional routes, for flights to the Caribbean (Cuba, Puerto Rico) and to Atlanta and Miami in the USA.

Depicted here is PJ-FHB, one of the carrier's FH-227s, in full ALM colours. The ICAO call sign is 'ANTILLEAN'.
(ALM-Antillean Airlines)

ANSETT AUSTRALIA (AN/AAA)   Australia

Ansett Australia can trace its origins back to 1936. On 17 February of that year, a Fokker Universal aircraft, equipped with six seats, took off from Hamilton bound for Melbourne. This was the birth of today's most important Australian domestic airline. Mr Reginald Myles Ansett, after whom the airline is called, also ran a flying school at Hamilton and offered weekend pleasure flights. On 14 April 1937, Ansett became a public company. A setback in the airline's history was a fire in 1939 that destroyed a hanger at Essendon with four Ansett aircraft inside. During World War II, most facilities were used for military purposes. Ansett survived the war period as an independent airline. In 1957, Australian National Airways, the biggest Australian carrier at that time, collapsed. The public was surprised when Ansett took over the rest of ANA after some months and changed its name to 'Ansett-ANA'. With this purchase, Ansett also acquired the majority holding in Butler Air Transport, N.S.W., later on Air N.S.W. and today operating under the brand-name 'Ansett Express'. In 1963 the airline bought a controlling shareholding in MacRobertson Miller Airlines, today Ansett West Australia. On 2 November 1964, the first jet, a Boeing B-727-100, entered service. Two years later the name Ansett-Airlines of Australia was adopted. In late 1979 the controlling majority of Ansett

passed to News Ltd and TNT (Thomas Nationwide Transport), which company is now the owner of Ansett. In 1981 the traditional red livery was changed and a new 'flying-stars' image was created, representing the stars of the Southern Cross. To replace the old Fokker F27s, in December 1984 Ansett ordered ten Fokker F50s, and thus was the launch customer of this type. In December 1990 Ansett changed its name into 'Ansett Australia' and introduced the current colour scheme, incorporating the Australian national flag in the tail design, substituting the flying stars. Some regional carriers that operated for Ansett — including East West Airlines in October 1993 — were renamed 'Ansett Express' and took the same livery. Today, Ansett Australia operates an ultramodern fleet of Boeing B-737-300s, Airbus A320s and Boeing B-767s. Its various commuter subsidiaries use Fokker F28s, BAe 146s and DHC 8s.

Top Here you see Ansett-Airlines of Australia Fokker F27-600 VH-FNT, in the company's very old, red colour scheme, with a matching black and red cheatline. *(Author's Collection)*

Bottom Depicted here in the 'flying-stars' livery with its all-white fuselage, you see Ansett's Fokker F27-200, VH-MMS, in summer 1987. The airline's ICAO call sign is 'ANSETT'. *(Author's Collection)*

AUSTRALIAN AIRLINES (TN/AUS)   Australia

For forty years, the airline was characterized by an impressive stability and profitability, until its name finally became extinct in November 1993. Formed by the Australian National Airlines Act in 1945, the airline's first flight was operated with a Douglas DC-3 between Melbourne and Sydney on 9 September 1946. The official name was TAA-Trans Australia Airlines with its operational base at Melbourne. Considerable expansion followed in 1949, when Qantas' local route-network was taken over. In 1960 TAA began international services to Papua New Guinea, which were discontinued in 1973 after Air Niugini had been established. In 1964 the jet age began for TAA with the introduction of Boeing B-727s. In the 1980s the fleet became standardized to Douglas DC-9-30s, Boeing B-727-200s and Airbus A300s. Some Fokker F27s still remained in service for regional services in the Australian north. The only international TAA route was a scheduled weekly service between Hobart (Tasmania) and Christchurch in New Zealand. In March 1985 TAA purchased 77.5 per cent of Air Queensland, which continued to operate separately for two years. For routes in West Queensland, where the Fokker F27 turned out to be too large, three BAe Jetstream 31s were delivered in 1986, but they remained in service

for only about two years. In July 1986 TAA was renamed 'Australian Airlines' and at the same time introduced a completely new logo with a wallaby on the tail. Until 1988 the airline was an efficiently-run and profitable state-owned carrier. The delivery of the ordered A320, however, had to be postponed, because the government planned to privatize Australian Airlines and thus did not allow the airline to increase its financial obligations. Despite this intervention, the jet fleet was modernized and standardized to Boeing B-737-300/400s and A300s, after the Boeing B-727 service had finally ended on 31 December 1992. In September 1992 Australian Airlines was taken over by and fully integrated into Qantas (Queensland and Northern Territories Aerial Services) until the end of October 1993. Qantas is the oldest Australian airline, founded in 1935, when the first international scheduled service from Brisbane to Singapore was inaugurated. Here you see Fokker F27-600, VH-TQS, sporting TAA's traditional colour scheme, in February 1984. In November 1989 the last Fokker F27s had been sold or leased to Air Spirit and Air North, but in summer 1990 three returned and were then operated under the name 'Australian Regional'. Australian Airline's ICAO call sign was 'AUSTRALIAN'. *(Author's Collection)*

AUSTRIAN AIR SERVICES (SO/AAS)   Austria

With an initial capital of 75 million Austrian Schilling, the airline was founded on 4 February 1980. Commercial flight activities began on 1 April 1980 with two Swearingen Metro IIs and one Cessna 414 on domestic routes linking Vienna, Salzburg, Graz, Klagenfurt and Linz. At the time of foundation the owners were the airports of Graz, Klagenfurt, Linz, Vienna and Salzburg (14.8 per cent each) and Austrian Airlines (26 per cent). Austrian Airlines took over the technical and operational handling of Austrian Air Services. In January 1981 the Cessna was withdrawn from use and a third Metro added to the fleet. The number of passengers carried was doubled by 1985 (45,500 passengers). On 19 June 1985, Austrian Airlines took over 100 per cent of Austrian Air Services (AAS). The company, however, was still operated separately. In early 1988, Austrian Air Services was the third airline worldwide to take over three Fokker F50s replacing the Metros, which were sold to TAT (France). Due to a delay in delivery, two Fokker F50s had to be leased from Ansett Australia in the beginning, both painted in full Austrian Air Services livery. In summer 1988 the first scheduled Austrian Air Services international flight operated between Klagenfurt and Frankfurt. Today the Fokker F50s are used on various minor international routes for Austrian Airlines, where the Douglas MD-80 proves to be too large. A fleet of eight Fokker F50s is presently maintained, two of which are still leased from Ansett Australia. The aircraft's colour scheme is similar to Austrian Airlines' livery. The tail is filled out by three broad beams coloured in red-white-red, thus representing Austria's national flag. Red 'Austrian' titles adorn the plain white fuselage underneath the windowline close to the front door. The red arrow, Austrian Airlines' logo, is applied beneath the cockpit and repeated in a tiny version on the engine, together with red 'Fokker 50' stickers.

Seen here during flight, Austrian Air Services' first Fokker F50, OE-LFA *Schwechat*, is portrayed. The airline's ICAO call sign is 'AIR SERVICES'. *(Austrian Airlines)*

AVIANCA COLOMBIA (AV/AVA)   Colombia

As Avianca's roots trace back to 5 December 1919, it is the oldest airline in the Americas and the world's second oldest airline still existing. On this day five Colombian and three German business-men came together with the public notary No. 2 of the circuit of Baranquilla to sign a certificate of incorporation of the 'Sociedad Colombo Alemana de Transportes Aereos, S.A.' (SCADTA). Even before that time some other entrepreneurs of Baranquilla had tried to call an airline into being but they had failed. Junkers Ju 13 float-planes started the first scheduled flights between Giradot (Bogota) and Baranquilla in 1921. Ten years later Pan American World Airways took over an eighty per cent holding in the airline. In 1940 SCADTA merged with Servicio Aereo Colombiano under the present name 'Avianca'. In 1954 Avianca took over the domestic carrier SAETA. Today further subsidiaries are Helicol and Sociedad Aeronautica de Medellin (SAM). In 1978 the airline finally bought back Pan Am's shares. The airline's home base is at Bogota-Eldorado Airport. Today eleven South and Middle American destin-ations are served: Guatemala, San Jose, Panama, San Andres, Quito, Guayaquil, Manaus, Lima, Rio de Janeiro, Santiago and Buenos Aires. In North America, Avianca operates scheduled flights to New York, Los Angeles and Miami, and the European destinations are Frankfurt, Madrid and Paris. During 1992 and 1993 Avianca completely modernized its fleet. Gradually all Boeing B-707 and Boeing B-727 aircraft were sold or withdrawn from use and replaced by Douglas MD-83 and Boeing B-757 jets. On the intercontinental routes the Boeing B-747 was substituted by two Boeing B-767-200s (Extended Range). In order to expand the domestic network within Colombia and to serve smaller airports, Avianca ordered six Fokker F50s in December 1992 and optioned on another four. The first Fokker F50 was delivered on 6 May 1993. This aircraft, PH-AVG, is here seen while passing through Miami on its way to Colombia. The airline's ICAO call sign is 'AVIANCA'. (Author's Collection)

BIRMINGHAM EUROPEAN AIRWAYS (VB/BEA)

United Kingdom

Founded on 1 March 1983, under the name 'Birmingham Executive Airways', the airline commenced flight operations between Birmingham and Zürich on 8 June 1983. The airline started with a fleet of three BAe 31 Jetstreams, linking Birmingham with Copenhagen, Geneva, Zürich and Milan. Soon routes were expanded to Amsterdam and Paris. In the 1984 winter schedule, Stuttgart and Stockholm appeared for the first time in the airline's network. In January 1986, Birmingham Executive returned its only Saab SF340 to the manufacturer and cancelled all further orders, due to many technical problems that had occurred with the type. Birmingham Executive Airways faced some trouble in 1988 as British Airways' competitive schedule on some European routes forced BEA to reduce prices. As a reaction, the airline introduced a programme called 'Country House Holidays' offering tickets combined with car rental firms and country guesthouses. In early 1989 TPL (The Plimsoll Line Ltd, i.e. Maersk Air Group) took over a minor share and Birmingham Executive Airways leased two Fokker F50s from Maersk for some of the busier routes to the continent. These included services to Amsterdam, Stuttgart and Paris-Charles de Gaulle and some flights for British Airways from Birmingham to Glasgow, Hamburg and Belfast. At the same time the name was changed to Birmingham European Airways (BEA). Both F50-turboprops were flown with Maersk Air crews and Danish registration. They were operated in bright blue basic Maersk Air colours and large BEA titles on the tail. On the underside, 'Birmingham European' titles interrupted the dark blue cheatline. In spring 1990 BEA began its first jet operations with the purchase of five ex-British Airways BAC 1/11-400s that had been stored at Bournemouth for some time. On 1 November 1992 Brymon Airways and Birmingham European Airways fused under the name 'Brymon European Airways' with the main operational base at Birmingham. Forty per cent were held by British Airways and 40 per cent by Maersk Air. But the airline had considerable losses and so in July 1993 Brymon European was divided again: British Airways took over 100 per cent of Brymon Airways and Maersk Air purchased 100 per cent of Birmingham European, which today operates under the name 'Maersk Air Ltd UK'. VB403 to Birmingham is here seen during take-off at Amsterdam's Schiphol Airport on 24 October 1989. Fokker F50, OY-MMV, displays full Maersk Air livery with Birmingham European titles. The airline's ICAO call sign was 'BIRMEX'. *(W. Kathe)*

BRIT AIR (DB/BZH)   France

The French regional carrier 'Brittany Air International' was formed in 1973 and acquired its first aircraft, two five-seat Piper Aztecs, in 1974. One year later the French Ministry of Transport licensed the Morlaix-based carrier as a 'Société de Transport Aérien Publique'; air taxi operations began and one Piper was based at Caen/ Normandie. In 1977 the Morlaix Chamber of Commerce and Industry acquired a 64 per cent controlling majority in Brit Air and one year later scheduled services started with the acquisition of two Embraer 110 Bandeirantes. First routes covered were Quimper-Morlaix-London and Caen-Le Havre-London, later also Morlaix-Jersey, Morlaix-Cork (Ireland) and the domestic route Rennes-Lyon. In addition to the airline's own scheduled and charter flights, a contract was made with Air Inter in 1983, to operate regularly between Quimper-Paris/Orly and Rennes-Paris/Orly for Air Inter. To cover these routes, Brit Air purchased two 50-seat Fokker F27-500s, which served until 1989, when they were sold to Federal Express. A new hangar was built at Morlaix to maintain the ordered Saab SF340 and ATR 42, a second followed in 1992. The newly-delivered first Saab SF340 entered service on the Lyon-Le Havre-

Caen route in early 1987. It displayed full Air France colours and also operated for Air France on European routes. The aircraft was replaced by Brit Air's own Saab SF340 in June 1987. In March 1989 Brit Air bought Europe Air, an EAS subsidiary and integrated fleet (Saab SF340s) and operations. Today, the fleet consists of twelve ATR 42s, three ATR 72s, six SF340s, and one last EMB 110. Forty-five per cent of the flights are operated under the airline's own name, 30 per cent for Air France and 25 per cent for Air Inter. Seen here at Lyon/Satolas Airport on 31 May 1986, Fairchild FH-227B, F-GCPU, is depicted in full Brit Air colours. This plane was leased from TAT for the Lyon-Rennes-Caen service for a short period. The airline's livery is inspired by colours and symbols of Brittany: beneath the cockpit, the disk-like yellow 'triskele' is displayed, a Celtic symbol representing the three elements of earth, water, and fire. The black 'Ermine' is Brittany's emblem, with both a yellow and a black cheatline underlining the windows and black 'Brit Air' titles applied in a bold typeface. Brit Air's ICAO call sign is 'BRITAIR'.
(W. Kathe)

BUSY BEE OF NORWAY (BS/BEE)   Norway

Busy Bee's history traces back to the year 1965, when the company was established under the name 'Busy Bee Airservice'. Between 1972 and 1980 the airline's official name was 'Air Executive Norway — Busy Bee', activities were maintained with Shorts Skyliner and Fokker F27 equipment and in 1981 the company was renamed 'Busy Bee of Norway A/S'. The airline was a subsidiary of L. G. Braathen Shipping Group, the owner of the oldest and most famous Norwegian air-carrier Braathens S.A.F.E., which was the main shareholder. In 1976/77 the last three Braathens S.A.F.E. F27s were taken over. Four more Fokker F27s were ordered in May 1985 plus one Boeing B-737-200, which was the only jet of Busy Bee's fleet. One F27 (LN-AKB) operated for the United Nations between February and May 1987 in neutralized colours. In 1988 the fleet increased to eleven Fokker F27s and one Boeing B-737-200. Busy Bee's activities included government contract flights and executive charters, but the main fields of operations were tour charter flights throughout Europe and scheduled passenger services carried out for Braathens S.A.F.E. and Scandinavian Airlines. The first Fokker F50 joined the fleet in September 1988, five were delivered altogether until the end of that year. In summer 1992 two Fokker F50s were leased to KLM City Hopper. These planes had to be returned in December the same year when the financial problems of the airline had accumulated and Busy Bee finally had to file its bankruptcy petition. A few months later Norwegian Air Shuttle was established as a successor company, operating three Fokker F50s. The other Fokker F50s were taken over by Vlaamse Luchttransport-Maatschappij, Antwerp.

Seen here while approaching Munich-Riem Airport on 18 October 1990, is Fokker F27-200, LN-AKA. Busy Bee's unique tail-logo was a cartoon-like, anthropomorphized, laughing and dancing bee, dressed up in a kind of striped shirt in yellow and black. In front of the rear door additional 'Bee-Liner' stickers can be seen. The airline's ICAO call sign was 'BUSYBEE'. *(W. Kathe)*

CONAIR AVIATION (CRC)   Canada

Conair Aviation Ltd is one of the largest Canadian air-companies, specializing in tanker operations. The company was originally formed in 1969 at Abbotsford, British Columbia, using such exotic types as CCF Harvard, DHC (Grumman) Tracker and Douglas A-26C Invaders. Since its early days, the company's specialities are forest fire water bombing and agricultural spraying services. Additionally, charter and contract aerial survey operations are carried out. Today a large fleet of over fifty aircraft is maintained. Cessna Turbo Centurion and Skymaster planes as well as Beechcraft Super King Air 200s are used for staff transport purposes. Seventeen Piper Aerostar 600s are busy with agricultural and survey operations, and for photo- and patrol-flights further Beechcraft 200s are in service. The extensive tanker fleet consists of Conair Firecats (modified and converted DHC CS2 Trackers), ten Douglas DC-6s and four Canadair CL-215 amphibians, which are operated by Yukon and N.W.T. governments. It is interesting that in addition, very specially converted Fokker F27 models were used for some years. On 6 June 1986, Conair got the type-certification for Fokker F27 operations and

the permission to use the first self-modified Fokker F27 as a sprayer aircraft (C-GSFS). The plane was mainly in action for forest fire combat. A second Fokker F27 (C-FBDY) was bought from Australian Airlines in March 1988. On 4 September 1989, the first converted water-bomber Fokker F27 C-CSFS crashed on a hill close to Arles in Southern France while operating for Sécurité Civile. The aircraft was replaced by another F27-600 (C-FGDS) that had been bought from Star Air/Denmark in November 1989. Both Fokker F27-600s, however, were sold to the French Sécurité Civile in June 1990. Here you can see the company's second F27-600, C-FBDY, in full Conair livery. The plane sports a basically white fuselage with a grey underside, separated by a broad red windowline that tapers beneath the fin. On the white tail, the fleet number of the aircraft is displayed in large red figures. The company's logo plus red 'Conair' lettering appear on the all-white cabin roof between front door and wing. Note the water-tank conversion, visible between the plane's undercarriage. Conair's ICAO call sign is 'CONAIR CANADA'. *(Author's Collection)*

CONTINENTAL AIRLINES
(CO/COA)
United States of America

Continental Airlines can trace its history back to 1934, when Varney Speed Airlines, Continental's predecessor, began operating between El Paso (Texas) and Pueblo (Colorado) with a Lockheed Vega. In May 1937 Wyoming Air Service's Denver-Pueblo route was taken over and the name changed to 'Continental Airlines'. The airline's base was transferred from El Paso to Denver. In 1955 Pioneer Air Lines was taken over, providing new hubs at Dallas and Austin. In 1963 headquarters were moved again, this time to Los Angeles. With the merger of Continental and Texas Air on 31 October 1982, the airline became one of America's biggest carriers. In September 1983 after a period of heavy losses, Continental filed for protection under Chapter 11, for the first time. Completely reorganized, a far smaller airline emerged from bankrupcty in 1986. In autumn 1986, Texas Air Holding integrated New York Air and Frontier Airlines into Continental. In November and December 1986 Continental purchased People Express and the Denver-based Rocky Mountain Airways, then operated for Continental Express throughout Colorado. In April 1987 the first DC-10 flight to Europe appeared in the Continental schedule, with the service from Denver to London Gatwick. With the integration of People Express, Britt Air had been taken over as well. This airline had a large fleet of Swearingen Metroliners and Fairchild F-27s that mainly operated for Continental Express in the area around Chicago and Detroit. As Royale Airlines from Houston/Texas suspended co-operation with Continental, three of Britt Air's F-27s were based at Houston, and used on services to Beaumont, College Station, Alexandria, Lafayette, Lake Charles, Laredo, Shreveport and Victoria. In March 1990, the company decided to merge Rocky Mountain Airways (Western Division) and Britt Air (Central Division) under the name Jet Link, with the main base of operation at Houston. In June 1990 the Fairchild F-27s were withdrawn from use. N380BA and N381BA, two of Britt Air's Houston-based Fairchild F-27Js, are here seen at Houston-Intercontinental Airport on 8 October 1988. They display Continental's traditional golden livery, with cheatlines in gold, red and orange. Black 'Continental Express' titles adorn the underside. In early 1991, however, Continental Airlines introduced a completely new colour scheme, with the three-dimensional quarter of a globe on the fin, represented by white degrees of latitude and golden degrees of longitude on an ocean-blue backdrop. A narrow golden stripe underlines both the windows and blue 'Continental' titles. The airline's ICAO call sign is 'CONTINENTAL'. *(W. Kathe)*

CROSSAIR (LX/CRX)   Switzerland

On 14 February 1975, the company was founded under the name "Business Flyers Basel AG" at Basle. In the beginning the fleet consisted of one Cessna 320 and a Piper J-4 Cub with two seats. The company leased out the planes or operated them on taxi flights and provided pilot training. During a visit to the USA, Moritz Suter, the airline's chief, studied the regional carrier Air Wisconsin and began working out if he could successfully establish a similar commuter airline in Central Europe. The Swiss Aviation Authority BAZL gave Business Flyers the certification for non-scheduled taxi services and the fleet was extended by further Cessna aircraft. The current name 'Crossair' was introduced on 14 November 1978. Three days later scheduled services from Zürich to Lyon, Luxembourg, Nürnberg, Innsbruck, Klagenfurt and Lugano were requested. The first regular flight with Swearingen Metroliner IIs started on 2 July 1979 to Nürnberg, Klagenfurt and Innsbruck. In 1982 a five-year contract of co-operation was signed by Crossair and Swissair, renewed in 1986, this time unlimited. Crossair was granted the exclusive rights for operation of planes with less than 40 seats and the current Crossair network was accepted. The schedules of both airlines were co-ordinated and Crossair was integrated into the reservation system of Swissair. In 1984 Crossair decided to build up a maintenance base at Basle, and leased a couple of F27s from DLT, WDL, and DAT due to technical problems with the engines of their newly-delivered Saab SF340s. In 1993 the new modern livery was presented: the fuselage is plain white with red and blue stripes. Behind the white Swiss cross on the red tail is a blue hook symbolizing 'Europe'. Today, six domestic and 38 international destinations are served. The fleet consists of Saab SF340A/Bs, Fokker F50s and BAe 146-200/300s (RJ85s). In 1994 the first Saab 2000 was delivered and the Fokker F50s will be returned to Fokker in 1995.

Depicted here on approach to Stuttgart Airport on 26 April 1992, Crossair's Fokker F50, HB-IAP, is seen in the airline's traditional livery. The white Swiss cross is displayed on an all-red tail, whereas the fuselage remains predominantly white, with two elegant lines below window level; one is coloured in blue, curving downwards at the front, the lower line in black, gradually fading into grey towards the rear part. The company's ICAO call sign is 'CROSSAIR'.
(W. Kathe)

DAT — DELTA AIR TRANSPORT (DE/DAT)

Belgium

Delta Air Transport is a Belgian regional commuter airline that provides air services to smaller places in Northern Central Europe. The airline was founded in 1966 by Freddy van Gaever, who had recently also founded VLM-Vlaamse Luchtvaart Maatschappij. For many years, five Fairchild FH-227Bs, had been the backbone of the company's flight activities, until they were finally sold in 1990. The airline operated international charter and contract flights from its base at Antwerp and provided feeder connections on shuttle flights to Amsterdam and Brussels for KLM's and Sabena's international networks. The FH-227s were also frequently leased to other airlines, and two FH-227s were leased out to Crossair in 1984. The planes additionally operated with Sabena on various international services and for Air France between Paris-Orly and Antwerp during the mid-1980s. In June 1987 the airline ordered three Embraer 120 Brasilias and optioned on another four to replace the Fairchild FH-227s. The first EMB 120 was delivered in June 1988. Two FH-227s were leased to ALM Antillean in May 1988 and replaced by an ex-Benin Government Fokker F28. In summer 1989, Delta Air Transport made an agreement with British Aerospace to take over two BAe 146-200s in autumn the same year. Today DAT has considerably expanded and maintains a fleet of nine Embraer 120 Brasilias, three Fokker F28s and seven BAe 146-200s. The company is now a fully-owned subsidiary of Sabena, and both the BAe 146s and F28s carry Sabena livery. DAT operates Sabena flights all around Central and Northern Europe using SN flight numbers.

Top As seen here on Delta Air Transport's Fairchild FH-227B, OO-DTB, the airline's current livery is just a copy of Sabena's traditional colour scheme, with a blue cheatline and blue tail being the backdrop for a white disk. Within this disk, DAT's delta-shaped company logo is displayed. The aircraft is here seen at Amsterdam-Schiphol taking off for flight HN393 to Antwerp. *(W. Kathe)*

Bottom Seen here at Antwerp-Deurne Airport on 18 September 1986, Delta Air Transport's Fairchild FH-227B, OO-DTE, is depicted in the company's old colour scheme. A broad three-tone blue cheatline runs along the fuselage at windowline to curve into the tail. Behind the cockpit it is interrupted by large 'DAT' titles, striped in blue. The company's delta-shaped logo is applied on the tail. DAT's ICAO call sign is 'DELTAIR'. *(W. Kathe)*

DLT (DW/DLT)   Germany

DLT's early history traces back to the year 1958, when Martin Decker and Jan Janssen founded 'OLT — Ostfriesische Lufttaxi' as a seaside resort air-service at Emden, Ostfriesland, the original predecessor of DLT. In 1973 the 'Aktiengesellschaft für Industrie- und Verkehrswesen' (AGIV) purchased the majority shareholding in OLT and a 20-seat DHC6 Twin Otter entered service. One year later, OLT changed its name into 'DLT Luftverkehrsgesellschaft mbH' and the operational base was transferred to Frankfurt. Regional services to Bayern, Hessen, Saarland and Nordrhein-Westfalen were built up, and in 1977 one Shorts SD330 was purchased. 1978 saw the first international DLT services along the Bremen-Copenhagen and Hannover-Amsterdam route, and closer co-operation with Lufthansa started after the German flag-carrier had acquired a 26 per cent interest in DLT. From 1981 on, the Hawker-Siddeley HS748 proved to be the carrier's backbone, operating scheduled services for Lufthansa. These turbo-props became especially famous, because they carried a flaming red livery covering the whole aircraft, including engines, all rudders and wheel-flaps. Between 1985 and 1988 a couple of WDL Fokker F27s were temporarily leased by DLT when required, sporting various liveries. In early 1985 DLT was one of the first airlines to order the new Fokker F50. The first Fokker F50 was delivered on 7 August 1987, entering service on the Hamburg-Brussels and Cologne-Copenhagen-Stuttgart route. For the summer schedule 1988, all regular DLT operations were changed into Lufthansa flights with LH/DLH codes. In March 1989 Lufthansa increased its participation in the airline and held a controlling majority of 52 per cent of DLT's capital. In December 1989 DLT decided to lease and later sell its whole Embraer 120 Brasilia fleet to Midway Airlines. In summer 1992 DLT was reorganized as 'Lufthansa City Line' to document that the company had become a full Lufthansa subsidiary.

Top Seen here at Düsseldorf Airport on 21 September 1986, Fokker F27-200, D-BAKU, is depicted while rolling-in on the taxiway. The aircraft sports the usual DLT livery of the mid-1980s, with its dark blue cheatline and tail with white DLT titles. *(W. Kathe)*

Bottom Depicted here during take-off at Frankfurt's Runway 18, West, on 5 May 1988, operating the scheduled flight to Saarbrücken, you see Fokker F50, PH-DMO, which was leased from Fokker for some months. The aircraft, with construction number 20103, is the third prototype and had an exceptional demonstrator colour scheme, a fully blue hind fuselage with an additional red diagonal streak in front. DLT's international call sign was 'DLT'. *(W. Kathe)*

On the inside front cover: Coming in on final approach to Munich-Riem Airport in the evening sun of 9 November 1990 you see Fokker F50 OY-MMU, in full DLT colours. The aircraft was leased from Maersk Air and had Danish registration. *(W. Kathe)*

FARNER AIR TRANSPORT (FAT)   Switzerland

Farner Air Transport was formed in 1984 as a subsidiary of Farner Aviation Holding, Grenchen. At that time Farner Aviation had been engaged in building and maintaining aircraft for sixty years. Farner Air Transport began operating several Cessnas on parcel express flights for TNT and Federal Express from its base at Basle and from Geneva to Brussels. In 1986 and 1987 additional regular flights for *The Wall Street Journal* were carried out between Maastricht/ Cologne and Basle. On the Basle-Brussels service, the Cessna was substituted by an Embraer 110 Bandeirante, leased from National Airways, U.K. From December 1987 on, a Cessna 404 was used for the UPS service from Basle to Cologne. On 1 July 1988, Farner Air Transport leased its first Fairchild F27J (F-GDXT) from Air Service Nantes to use it on the scheduled Fedex service Geneva-Basle-Brussels. The leasing ended in November 1988 and the Fairchild was replaced by a Fokker F27 leased from Servisair, Belgium and flown by Farner pilots until early 1990. The leased Fokker F27 was replaced by two own F27s, bought in March and November 1990.

The Bandeirante mainly flies for Emery Worldside between Maastricht, Basle and Bergamo. In 1991 two Pilatus Porters and one DHC 6 Twin Otter joined the fleet to serve for the United Nations' Swiss Medical Unit in West Sahara. These services still continue. In 1992 Balair, up to then maintaining the Farner Air Transport fleet, had to cancel the contract and FAT took over Air Service Basel AG, which today works as a Farner subsidiary for maintenance. In December 1993 the airline purchased another ex-Air France Fokker F27 (F-BPUI) to operate it for Federal Express between Cologne and Geneva. At the same time Farner Air Transport bought Nawa Air Transport, Hungary, operating with Let 410s and Fokker F27s. Depicted here on the tarmac at Berne-Belp, is Fokker F27-400, HB-ITQ, the only F27 that ever had full 'Farner Air Transport' titles on an all-white fuselage. On the fin, the obligatory Swiss cross is displayed. The company's ICAO call sign is 'FARNER'. *(Author's Collection)*

FEDERAL EXPRESS (FM/FDX)

United States of America

Federal Express was the first airline in the USA to start specializing on parcel and cargo pick-up and delivery services in April 1973. With lorries and 32 Falcon F20 jets, Federal Express established an overnight delivery service between 48 places in the USA and their home base at Memphis. Due to air cargo deregulation in 1977 Federal Express was permitted to operate larger planes; they consequently bought a couple of old ex-United Airlines Boeing B-727-22s and installed cargo doors. In April 1978 Federal Express became a publicly-held company and is listed on the New York Stock Exchange since 28 December 1978. Until 1984 the fleet gradually expanded and ten Douglas DC-10s, 15 Boeing B-727-200s, 35 Boeing B-727-100s and 24 Falcon F20s were operated at that time. For fast deliveries to small airfields 30 one-prop Cessna Caravans were ordered that year. Until 1992 the total number of delivered Cessna Caravans increased to 216 units altogether. The five ex-Air Inter Fokker F27s that operated on the European network for a very short period in early 1988 were then transferred to the USA. In October 1988 Fedex made a contract with Fokker to purchase 20 Fokker F27s, consisting of eleven ex-Malaysian Airlines and nine

ex-Scandinavian aircraft, returned to Fokker after delivery of the new Fokker F50s to these companies. Today Federal Express operates 32 Fokker F27s, eight of them belong to the 600 series, the remaining planes are F27-500s with a maximum useful load of 19,300 lb. In February 1989, Fedex took over and integrated Flying Tiger Airlines (Tiger International) the world's oldest freight airline. Fedex began European regional services on 21 December, 1989, using a BAF/Servisair Fokker F27 in white Fedex colours. In July 1991 Federal Express ordered 25 Airbus A300-600 freighters for delivery as from 1994 to replace the Boeing B-747s the company had to take over when Flying Tigers was integrated. Today the company serves 186 countries in all continents.

OO-FEA, a Fokker F27-600, can be seen here on the tarmac of Frankfurt Airport on 16 October 1990. Like the other F27s it has been operated in an all white livery with big blue/red 'FEDEX' titles on the rear sector of the fuselage and small 'Europe' titles below. The USA-based F27s have 'Feeder' titles instead. *(W. Kathe)*

The airline's ICAO call sign is 'EXPRESS'.

FINNAIR (AY/FIN) Finland

Finland's national carrier Finnair can look back over 70 years. It was originally formed in 1923 under the name Aero Oy by the flying pioneer Bruno Lucander. Finnair's first flight took off on 20 March 1924, from Helsinki to Tallinn in the Baltic republic of Estonia. At that time a four-seat Junkers plane was used. After World War II, the airline was renamed 'Aero-Finnish Air Lines', later on 'Finnair'. Today, the Finnish Government holds 76 per cent in the airline, the remaining 24 per cent are bank, insurance, and investment interests. Finnair itself has controlling majority in Finnaviation, a Finnair subsidiary, and a one hundred per cent holding in its charter subsidiary Karair. Today an extensive domestic network is maintained by Finnair, Finnaviation and Karair. International Finnair services include all important European centres, North America, North Africa and the Far East. After the withdrawal of the SE210 Caravelle and the DC-8 in the early 1980s, the fleet became standardized to DC-9-40/50s, MD-80s and DC-10s. In the late 1970s Finnair decided to replace its old piston-engined Convair 440s by Fokker F27s. In April 1980 the first two F27-200s were taken over from Icelandair, a third followed in early 1982. Technical support for the 44-seat F27s was firstly entrusted to Karair and later to Icelandair. As the F27s soon both proved to be too large for some

routes and too old in the long term, Finnair decided to operate Finnaviation's Embraer 110 Bandeirantes and Saab SF340s on minor routes and to order four ATR 42s, in 1982, for delivery after March 1986. In summer 1987 the two remaining Fokker F27s were stored at Helsinki. In 1985 five ATR 72s were ordered and delivered to Karair in 1990 and 1991. The five ATR 42s were given in part payment, when the ATR 72s had been delivered. In late 1986 and early 1987 two Airbus A300s joined the Karair fleet, but they are now in service for Finnair in full such colours. Today, the aging DC-10 long-haul fleet is gradually being replaced by MD-11s. Depicted here on the tarmac of Helsinki's Vantaa Airport in July 1982, you see Fokker F27-200, OH-LKC. This aircraft was built in 1964 and delivered to All Nippon Airways, Japan. A few years later it went to the Icelandic Coast Guard; it was then leased to Libyan Arab Airlines where it was heavily damaged in 1981. After its repair at Icelandair's maintenance centre, it was purchased by Finnair, where it remained in service until summer 1987. After over a year of storage, in late 1988 the F27 was bought by Sunshine Aviation and re-registered HB-ISH. In late 1993 the aircraft was stored again, after Sunshine's merge with Air Engiadina. Finnair's ICAO call sign is 'FINNAIR'.
(Author's Collection)

ICELANDAIR (FI/ICE)   Iceland

The company was originally founded on 3 June 1937 under the name Akureyri Air/Flugfelag Akureyrar. The airline's first regular flight was operated by a five-seat Waco float-plane between Akureyri and Reykjavik on 29 April 1938. Two years later the name was changed to Icelandair/Flugfelag Islands. The Douglas DC-3 was the first large aircraft operated; in 1948 DC-4s and later Vickers Viscounts joined the fleet. The Fokker F27 was introduced in 1965 and the Boeing B-727, Icelandair's first jet, in 1967. On 1 August 1973, Icelandair / Flugfelag Islands and Loftleidir merged under the name Icelandair. Loftleidir had also operated DC-4s and DC-6s in its old days and maintained a fleet of Canadair CL44s and Douglas DC-8s at the time of fusion. The standardized Icelandair fleet of the 1980s consisted of five Fokker F27 for domestic services, two Boeing B-727-100 and -200 series each, for the European services and a various number of Douglas DC-8s (series 33, 55 and 63) for the transatlantic routes. These cheap flights to the USA are a traditional part of the airline's operations. The first DC-4 flight took off at Luxembourg-Findel on 22 May 1955 bound for Gander and New York. Luxembourg has been the European base for these transatlantic flights ever since. Due to the 'open sky' policy and the tougher competition on the North American market, the airline had to face financial problems between 1979 and 1983, when DC-10s and B-747s were operated on short-term lease to keep up a minimum of transatlantic services. After Air Bahama, an Icelandair subsidiary, was shut down, the airline gradually regained a foothold. Icelandair became one hundred per cent privately owned in autumn 1985. The largest single shareholder presently is Eimskip, an Icelandic shipping company, holding 34 per cent of the company's shares. Today Icelandair has one of the most modern fleets, operating Fokker F50s, Boeing B-737-400s and Boeing B-757s. At the moment Washington, Orlando, Fort Lauderdale and New York are served in the USA, and European services include nineteen destinations. The company's livery consists of a window-line in dark blue and a blue tail motif showing two waves that form the initial 'F' of Flugleidir on the port side and the mirror image opposite. Here you can see Fokker F27-200, TF-FLN, depicted at Akureyri in summer 1990. The domestic aircraft sport large 'Flugleidir' titles and small Icelandair stickers behind the wing. The Fokker F50s serve ten domestic airports and the international route to Glasgow via the Faroes, regularly. Icelandair's ICAO call sign is 'ICEAIR'. *(Author's Collection)*

ISLENA AIRLINES (WC/ISV)   Honduras

Islena Airlines was formed in 1982 under the name 'Islena de Inversiones, SA de CV' at La Ceiba. In its early days, Cessna 185 Skywagons, Cessna 206 Stationairs, Piper Apaches and Pilatus BN-2A Islanders were operated on charter and taxi flights. The first large plane was a de Havilland DHC 6 Twin Otter purchased in the late 1980s. In July and September 1990 two Embraer 110 Bandeirantes were leased from Pal Air and Pacestar for scheduled domestic operations. The first Fairchild F-27F (a converted A-version) was bought in July 1991 and exactly one year later, the Honduran airline purchased two more Fairchild F-27s which had flown for Airlift (USA) before and had been stored at Miami for months. Scheduled flights are mainly operated between Tegucigalpa and La Ceiba, but also to international destinations in Middle America, like Guatemala and Mexico. After all the smaller aircraft were sold,

the fleet became standardized to two Beechcraft 99 Airliners, three Embraer 110 Bandeirantes and three Fairchild F-27s in 1993. Additionally, a Shorts SD360 was bought from Air Wisconsin in June 1993. Depicted here on the tarmac at Miami International Airport in October 1992, you can see Islena's Fairchild F-27F, HR-IAH, in the airline's full livery. A bright blue cheatline runs along the windowline, an oceanic blue and a thin black stripe below. They all taper to the nose. This arrangement is repeated in the middle of the fin, beneath the company's logo: a sphere standing for the globe, with tiny blue waves at the bottom and an azure sky above, with two palm trees on an island and a white goose-like bird before a dark orange sun on top. Soft black 'Islena' titles are applied behind the cockpit. The international ICAO call sign is 'ISLENA'. *(Author's Collection)*

JERSEY EUROPEAN AIRLINES (JY/JEA)

United Kingdom/Jersey

Jersey European Airlines' true history began on 1 November 1979, when the company was formed to take over the activities of Intra Airways, which had been founded in 1969. Operations started with a fleet of Piper PA-31 Navajos, Pilatus BN-2A Islanders, Embraer 110 Bandeirantes and de Havilland DHC 6 Twin Otters. Scheduled passenger flights between Jersey and the British mainland and to France were offered. Early destinations were London-Gatwick, Stansted and Shoreham in Britain and Dinard and Paris in France. In January 1986 two more Embraer Bandeirantes were bought from Valdez Airlines. They were also used on the new services from Belfast Harbour Airport to Birmingham. In March 1988 the first two Fokker F27s were bought for pax flights. In September 1988 Jersey European got traffic rights for a scheduled Jersey-Birmingham service which was operated in competition with British Midland using a Fokker F27. Another competing service was the Jersey-Guernsey-Southampton route, where Air UK was already in business. In September 1989 the first HS 748 was delivered to Jersey European. Altogether three units of this type were operated, but returned in summer 1990. As a replacement, six Fokker F27s were

bought from the Australian East West Airlines. In November 1989, Royal Mail decided to accept Jersey European as a partner for night-post operations out of Luton with a couple of Shorts SD330 and SD360. In March 1993 Jersey European leased three BAe 146s for charter flights and for the services from London to Jersey and Belfast to London City. Today, Jersey European's fleet consists of one Embraer 110 Bandeirante, four Shorts SD360s, eight Fokker F27-500s and three BAe 146-200/300s. The domestic network includes Belfast, Birmingham, Blackpool, Bournemouth, Bristol, Exeter, Guernsey, Isle of Man, Jersey, Leeds, London-Gatwick, Manchester and Southampton. International destinations are Dinard and Paris. Here, Fokker F27-500, G-JEAD, can be admired on the final stage of approach to Belfast Harbour Airport on 5 October 1992. The aircraft came on flight JY840 from Bristol. It displays the company's current livery, with its all white fuselage, 'Jersey European' titles underneath the windowline and the company's colourful logo both behind the cockpit and in the tail. The airline's ICAO call sign is 'JERSEY'.
(W. Kathe)

KLM — ROYAL DUTCH AIRLINES (KL/KLM)   Netherlands

KLM is the world's oldest airline, whose name has remained unchanged for 75 years. The airline was founded on 7 October 1919 under the full name 'N.V. Koninklijke Luchtvaart Maatschappij voor Nederland en Kolonien' by the Dutch military pilot Albert Plesman. Two passengers joined the first regular KLM flight, that took off on 17 May 1920 at London-Croydon bound for Amsterdam. The de Havilland DH 16 used on this flight was leased from Air Transport and Travel Ltd. KLM's first own aircraft were de Havilland DH9s and Fokker F.IIs, operating to Paris, Brussels and Bremen. KLM's first long-haul flight started on 4 October 1924, when a Fokker F.VIIa took off from Amsterdam heading for Batavia (today Jakarta) in the Dutch colony of Indonesia. The 14,000 km flight took 51 days. In 1929 KLM began operating regularly on this route every fortnight with Fokker F.VIIbs, (later Douglas DC-2s), thus being the world's longest scheduled route until World War II. A dark chapter in KLM's history was 10 May 1940, when German troops bombed Amsterdam-Schiphol Airport and most KLM planes were irreparably destroyed, except for some DC-3s which survived in England. At that time KLM got four Douglas DC-5s, being the only airline that ever operated this type. After the war, KLM quickly expanded and served over eighty cities in fifty countries and all continents by 1951.

A large fleet of Douglas DC-3s, DC-4s, DC-6s, DC-7s, Lockheed Constellations, Convair 240/340s and Vickers Viscounts was maintained during the 1950s. In 1961 the jet age began for KLM with the delivery of the first DC-8-50. Today a fleet of Douglas DC-10s, Boeing B-737-200/300/400s, Boeing B-747-300/400s, Airbus A310s and Fokker F100s is operated. In early December 1993, KLM took over the first MD-11 that will replace the old DC-10s. In May 1988 Netherlines became a 100 per cent subsidiary of KLM as well. To replace the old NLM Fokker F27s, KLM ordered seven and optioned on three Fokker F50s for delivery after 1990. Netherlines' Jetstreams were gradually replaced by twelve Saab SF340s as from 1990. On 1 April 1991, KLM City Hopper was formed out of NLM City Hopper and Netherlines. A modern fleet of Fokker F50s, Saab SF340s and Fokker F28s, which are going to be replaced by Fokker F100s, is maintained.

Fokker F50, PH-KVH, is here seen on approach to Stuttgart-Echterdingen on 26 April 1992. The livery shown is a simple white body and a dark blue tail with diagonally applied, white 'cityhopper' titles. 'KLM Cityhopper' lettering appears behind the front door. The ICAO call signs are 'KLM' and 'CITY'. *(W. Kathe)*

LADECO (UC/LCO)   Chile

Ladeco was formed in summer 1959 with the intention to link Santiago with the copper mining area in north Chile. That's why the airline's acronym stands for 'Línea Aérea del Cobre' or 'Copper Airlines'. Flight operations started on 1 November 1958, with a Douglas DC-3 on the route from Santiago to El Salvador. Soon afterwards a second DC-3 was added, later followed by DC-6s. Gradually operations extended to all principal cities in the country. In 1975 the jet age began for Ladeco, when a Boeing B-727 was purchased to replace the DC-6 fleet. It had taken nearly 20 years, before the first international services commenced in 1978 with regular flights to Asuncion (Paraguay) and São Paolo (Brazil), with the flight being extended to Rio de Janeiro the following year. In 1982 Mendoza (Argentina), Guayaquil (Ecuador) and Bogota (Colombia) appeared in Ladeco's schedule. Scheduled services to Miami with Boeing B-727-100s started on 9 July 1983. In April 1990 two older Boeing B-727-100s were sold to UPS and replaced by Boeing B-737-200s. At the same time Ladeco decided to lease two Boeing B-757s from ILFC to operate on the services to Miami and New York instead of the Boeing B-707s. In December 1992 Ladeco replaced its Boeing B-707 freighter with a DC-8-71. Today,

Washington, Mexico, Havana, San Jose and Buenos Aires are additional international destinations. The current fleet consists of Boeing B-707s, B-727-100s, B-737-200/300s, B-757s, BAC 1/11s and one Douglas DC-8 freighter. The BAC 1/11s and B-737s are mainly used on the domestic network including thirteen destinations. In early 1988 Ansett Australia bought 25 per cent of Ladeco and today 35 per cent are held by the Spanish flag-carrier Iberia. Here you see Fokker F27-500, CC-CIS, in the airline's old livery. An orange and a yellow cheatline runs along the white fuselage and extends to the tail. The company's logo, a white 'L' on a black disk, is displayed on the front part of the fin. The two Fokker F27-500Fs were purchased from Air N.S.W. (Australia) for domestic services in December 1987, but they remained in the fleet for only about three years. In November 1990 Ladeco bought two BAC 1/11s from Dan Air London as a replacement for the two Fokker F27s. Both were sold to Espresso Aereo SA, Peru in September 1991. In summer 1990, Ladeco introduced a new colour scheme with a plain white fuselage and one yellow and blue triangle. Ladeco's ICAO call sign is 'LADECO'. *(Author's Collection)*

LANDHELGISGAEZLA ISLANDS (ICG)   Iceland

The Fokker F27 served not only as passenger or cargo plane for airlines or parcel services or — in its military version — for the airforces of various countries, but occasionally had also to take over very special tasks, like the service for Landhelgisgaezla Islands. Behind this name stands the Icelandic Coast Guard, which is not a military department or organization but a Government Patrol and Rescue organization. The 'company' was already founded in 1926. The main task is the survey of the long and rocky Icelandic coast. This is mainly carried out by various helicopters, like the Hughes 369D, which has been in service since 1981, an Aérospaciale AS350B Ecureuil and an Aérospaciale AS365N Dauphin 2. Additionally, in the mid-1970s two Fokker F27-200s were purchased. The F27 is mainly used on survey-flights at a height of about 300 feet along the coast. The aircraft that is still in service is equipped with two radar sets and scanners for surface-detection. Violations of the Icelandic territorial waters are reported to the nearest patrol boat of the Coast Guard. Due to large accessory tanks, the aircraft is able to fly for about 20 hours without refuelling. Nearly daily, the Fokker F27 is used on supervisional flights which normally take a few hours. The livery consists of a thick red windowline that becomes narrower beneath the cockpit, a dark blue and a thin red line that cross the fuselage diagonally between the wings and tail and a pennant-shaped Icelandic flag in the tail. The Fokker F27-200 TF-SYN is depicted here on the tarmac at Reykjavik Airport in July 1990. The international call-sign is 'ICELAND COAST'.
(Author's Collection)

LIBYAN ARAB AIRLINES (LN/LAA)   Libya

In 1964 Libyan Arab was formed under the name 'Kingdom of Libya Airlines', a government corporation, succeeding NAA Libiavia. But five years later, in September 1969, Muammar al Qaddafi overthrew King Idris' monarchy and the Libyan Arab Jamahiriya was founded. The name of the carrier was changed into 'Jamahiriya Libyan Arab Airlines' at the same time. The airline is fully state-controlled and operates an extensive domestic network and international European flights to Amsterdam, Athens, Belgrade, Berlin, Bucharest, Frankfurt, Istanbul, Larnaca, London, Madrid, Malta, Milan, Moscow, Paris, Rome, Sofia, Vienna, Warsaw and Zürich. Additionally, several places in North Africa and the Middle East were served, like Algiers, Amman, Casablanca, Damascus, Jeddah, Karachi, Kuwait, Sfax, and Tunis. The airline, however, is still strongly affected by various embargos. So, Boeing B-737s, B-747SPs and B-767 aircraft have been ordered, but they were unable to be delivered due to a trading embargo of the USA. The delivery of Airbus equipment has been blocked as well. Nevertheless, two ex-Caledonian Airbus A310s found their way to Libya in 1987, but they could not enter regular service due to a lack of spares. Finally they were sold to Air Algerie. The A310s, however, operated again for Libyan Arab Airlines in winter 1991/92. The aircraft carried Air Algerie titles, but had LAA basic colours and were flown by Libyan crews. An A300-600 was additionally leased from Egypt Air during that winter season. In March 1992 the operations of Jamahiriya Air Transport were finally integrated into Libyan Arab Airlines. Since 15 April 1992, no regular flights to international destinations were permitted, as a consequence of the U.N. sanctions against Libya. So the fleet of Boeing B-707s, B-727s, Ilyushin Il-76 freighters, Lockheed Hercules, Fokker F27s and F28s is stored, except for a couple of planes used on domestic flights. Here you see Fokker F27-600, 5A-DBT, on the apron of Zürich-Kloten Airport in September 1991. The aircraft sports full Libyan Arab Airlines colours, a broad cheatline in a blend of brown and gold, bending downwards below cockpit and nose. The dark brown tail logo, representing the Uaddan, a North African species of deer, is displayed on the all-golden-brown tail within a white disk. Centrally beneath the windowline of the port side, Arabic Libyan Arab Airlines titles are applied. The airline's ICAO call sign is 'LIBAIR'. *(Author's Collection)*

LUFTHANSA CITY LINE (CL/CLH)   Germany

If you try to trace back Lufthansa City Line's history you will end up in the year 1958, when 'OLT-Ostfriesische Lufttaxi' was founded. It took some 16 years until the company was renamed 'DLT Luftver-kehrsgesellschaft mbH', which is the actual predecessor of Lufthansa City Line. In the beginning, one DHC 6 Twin Otter flew on regional services and in 1977 the first Shorts SD330 was purchased. Up to then, the airline had been operating quite independently, which changed one year later when Lufthansa took over its first 26 per cent interest in DLT. Flights were operated for Lufthansa and in 1984 most routes were offered under LH/DLH flight numbers. In 1987 DLT was one of the first airlines to get the new Fokker F50 delivered. Two years later, Lufthansa acquired a 52 per cent controlling interest in the airline and the fleet became standardized to Fokker F50, after all Hawker-Siddeley HS748s and Embraer 120 Brasilias had been taken out of service. On 25 October 1992 the first Canadair RJ-100 Regional Jet entered service for Lufthansa, because in March 1992, DLT had finally ceased to exist and was renamed 'Lufthansa City Line'. A completely new logo, somewhat resembling the Lufthansa emblem, was created and within a few months the whole fleet shone in the new livery. The fuselage was still all-white, with 'Lufthansa City Line' titles in dark blue. On a blue fin, a thin yellow circle with four stripes formed the less innovative logo. This colour scheme, however, was changed again after not even one year. Today, the aircraft display full Lufthansa colours, with the well-known blue crane within a yellow disk on a blue tail. In early 1994 the amalgamation trend continued, when Lufthansa decided to give up the name 'Lufthansa City Line' after less than two years. In future all commuter aircraft will carry full Lufthansa livery and titles. Prior to that, Lufthansa had also integrated German Cargo into Lufthansa Cargo in May 1993, and the aircraft — including the DC-8s — were repainted. Today a large commuter fleet of Fokker F50s and Canadair Regional Jets is maintained and for some services turboprops from partner airlines, as Contactair DHC 8 and Cimber ATR 42, are leased. Lufthansa intends to wind down these contracts.

Top Fokker F50, D-AFKL, is here seen at Cologne on 27 May 1992, still sporting Lufthansa City Line's first livery. The airline's ICAO call sign is 'HANSALINE'. *(W. Kathe)*

Bottom Lufthansa City Line's Fokker F50, D-AFKW, is here seen on the tarmac at Geneva-Cointrin Airport on 19 May 1993, in its new livery with Lufthansa tail logo. *(W. Kathe)*

LUXAIR (LG/LGL)

The airline was founded in 1961. On 2 April 1962, the first Fokker F27 took off for its flight from Luxembourg to Paris, shortly afterwards scheduled services to Frankfurt and Amsterdam were introduced. In its earlier days the airline operated Lockheed Constellations, Starliners, Aérospaciale Caravelles, Vickers Viscounts and Boeing B-707s. On 31 December 1984, the last Boeing B-707 was replaced by an Airbus A300B4; the aircraft was leased from Lux. Aviation Investment and operated on behalf of Luxavia for its scheduled service to Johannesburg via Nairobi. The main Luxair shareholders are the State of Luxembourg, the Luxembourg Steel Industry, the broadcasting station RTL, Luxair Finance SA and several banks and private shareholders. In summer 1986 the airline founded Luxair Commuter SA for regional flights within the Benelux states and to places in France and Germany. Two Swearingen Metroliner IIIs were taken into service for that purpose. Further subsidiaries are Luxair Tours, Luxair Executive and additionally Luxair participates in Cargolux. Since its early days the number of passengers has been gradually increasing from about 12,000 to 369,000 annual passengers in 1985. Nowadays tourism makes about 40 per cent of Luxair's total returns, and that is why many charter destinations in the Mediterranean, various Greek islands and the Canary Isles are seasonally served on scheduled flights. During the recent four years the fleet was totally modernized. It now consists of four Fokker F50 turboprops that had replaced the Fokker F27s between 1989 and 1991, two Boeing B-737-400s (in 1992), two Boeing B-737-500s (joined the fleet in 1993) and one Boeing B-747SP, that replaced the A300 in late 1987. This Boeing B-747SP is leased from South African Airways/Trans Lease International Ltd. and operates for Luxavia on the service to Johannesburg. From late 1993 on, these services are marketed under the traditional name 'Trek Air' and the flights now regularly stop at Munich. The fleet of Luxair Commuter SA consists of four Embraer Brasilias which had superseded the Metroliners in 1991. Luxair's colour scheme uses the Grand Duchy's national flag colours. A distinctive blue colours both the broad cheatline and the tail. There, the airline's half-arrow logo is displayed in white, usually pointing forward. The Fokker F27s were painted in a modified livery with a white fin and blue company motif.

Fokker F50, LX-LGC *Prince Guillaume*, can here be admired in its very final stage of approach to Luxembourg-Findel Airport on 28 August 1992. The airline's ICAO call sign is 'LUXAIR'. *(W. Kathe)*

MAERSK AIR (DM/DMA)   Denmark

The airline is part of the multi-group A. P. Möller, which is one of the largest and richest companies in Scandinavia, mainly concentrating in shipping. The airline was established in February 1969 and started flight operations in December. In 1970 Falckair was absorbed and in November 1971 Maersk Air, SAS and Cimber Air created 'Danair', Denmark's domestic scheduled air-carrier. In those days a fleet of Hawker Siddeley 748s, Boeing B-720s and Boeing B-737-200s operated on scheduled domestic and international charter flights. Today, after Sterling's fall, Maersk Air is the leading independent Danish airline. Three Bell 212s and three Super Puma helicopters are used in the oil business, and one HS 125 is operated for general business purposes (each in full colours). Additionally to Maersk's own charter and scheduled operations, some planes are regularly used on Danair's domestic Danish services. Due to liberalization of the European market, Maersk was able to start scheduled international services in late 1984. The first route introduced was Billund-Southend, operated with a de Havilland Canada Dash 7 twice a day. In autumn 1987, the company's DHC 7s were replaced by the first four Fokker F50s. In

September 1987 A.P. Möller Group founded Star Air as a 100 per cent Maersk subsidiary operating ex-Alkair F27s on cargo and passenger charters. In October 1988 Maersk Air took over a minority share in Brymon Airways. After disintegration of Brymon European in 1993, Maersk Air took its separate part and renamed it 'Maersk Air Ltd. (UK)'. Today the airline operates a fleet of Boeing B-737-300/400/500s, Fokker F50s, BAe 125s, Aérospaciale Super Puma and Dauphin helicopters; Star Air maintains four Fokker F27s and Maersk Air UK has a fleet of BAC 1/11-400/500s and BAe 31 Jetstreams. Scheduled domestic services run between Copenhagen and Billund, Esbjerg, Odense, Roenne and Vojens; international scheduled activities include the Copenhagen-London and Faroe Islands route, as well as Billund-Amsterdam, Brussels, Faroe Islands, Frankfurt, London and Stockholm. Depicted here at Cologne on 3 May 1989, you see Fokker F50, OY-MMG, in Maersk Air's traditional livery. Maersk Air is the first European customer of the Boeing B-737-X, the delivery of which will start in spring 1997. The airline's ICAO call sign is 'MAERSKAIR'. *(W. Kathe)*

MALAYSIA AIRLINES (MH/MAS)   Malaysia

The actual predecessor of Malaysia Airlines was founded in late 1937 by the Straits Steamship Company under the name 'Malayan Airways Ltd' with BOAC (British Overseas Airways Corporation) as its main shareholder, but it lasted ten years until the airline's maiden flight took off. A fleet of Airspeed Consuls and Douglas DC-3s was maintained in the beginning; during the 1950s and early 1960s Douglas DC-4s, Bristol Britannias (leased from BOAC), Lockheed Super Constellations (leased from Qantas) and Comet 4s joined the fleet. With the formation of the state of Malaysia in 1963, the airline was renamed 'Malaysian Airlines' and the first Fokker F27s were added to the fleet. Three years later the governments of both Malaysia and Singapore acquired a majority shareholding in the airline. The fleet became gradually enlarged by adding Boeing B-707 and B-737 jet equipment. After Singapore's separation from Malaysia, the airline was renamed 'Malaysia-Singapore Airlines' (MSA) on 1 January 1967. The tensions between the two states, however, were too evident and fundamental and so the airline was split again. On 3 April 1971, Malaysian Airlines System was officially founded and on 1 October 1972 it finally took over the Malaysian part of the old MSA operations. The fully state-owned company started off with a mixed fleet of nine Fokker F27s, seven Boeing B-737s and three Britten Norman Islanders. In September 1984, the Malaysian government decided to launch a programme for privatization of MAS. Today, 48 per cent is privately held, the Malaysian Ministry of Finance holds a 42 per cent and the two federal states Sarawak and Sabah a 5 per cent share each. Malaysian Airline Systems's acronym MAS, which is the Malayan word for 'gold', revealing the quality of the airline's service, was changed into 'Malaysia Airlines' in November 1987 and the airline introduced the current livery. It consists of a modernized version of the Malaysian symbol — the dragon Kelatan — as a tail-logo and a red and blue cheatline broadening and curving downwards beneath the fin. Today a fleet of DHC 6 Twin Otters, Fokker F50s, Boeing B-737-200/300/400s and 500 series, Boeing B-747-200/300/400s, Airbus A300s and Douglas DC-10s is operated. Here you see the airline's first Fokker F50, 9M-MGA, after its delivery in September 1989. The F50s are based at Kuala Lumpur, Kota Kinebalu and Kuching, shared amongst the three airports. The carrier's ICAO call sign is 'MALAYSIAN'. *(Malaysia Airlines)*

MERPATI NUSANTARA AIRLINES (MZ/MNA)   Indonesia

Merpati Nusantara is today the second largest Indonesian airline. Its history traces back to 6 September 1992, when the airline was founded with assistance from the Indonesian Airforce. One week later the first flight commenced between Jakarta and Kalimantan. When Indonesia gained its full independence from the Netherlands in 1963, Merpati was given responsibility to build up an effective network of domestic air transport. Many new pioneer routes were opened during the 1960s and 1970s and the fleet of Vickers Viscounts, Vickers Vanguards, Hawker Siddeley 748s and DHC 6 Twin Otters steadily grew. On 28 October 1978, Garuda, Indonesia's national carrier, assumed control over the airline, which therefore became government-controlled. In June 1986 Merpati ordered fifteen CASA CN235 Nurtanios for delivery between December 1986 and early 1991. After some initial troubles the first CASAs were taken into service in early 1988. In September 1986 Merpati replaced its last Vickers Vanguard (sold to EAS/France for parts) with two Lockheed Hercules. One year later, Merpati Nusantara leased two Fokker F28s, the airline's first jets, from Garuda for the route Denpasar-Kupang-Darwin (Australia). The service had formerly been flown by the airline's two HS 748s. In early 1988 a new livery with a modernized white body style and a deep blue tail with three interrupted, diagonal yellow waves was unveiled and the

airline's name changed into 'Merpati'. In January 1990, most domestic routes were transferred from Garuda to Merpati and so the company took over fifteen Fokker F28s from Garuda. Due to governmental intervention, Merpati had to take over the options for twelve Fokker F100s from the Garuda order in September 1992. On 27 September 1993 the first Fokker F100 was delivered. The current Merpati fleet consists of ten CASA Aviocars, fourteen CASA 235s, ten DHC 6 Twin Otters, thirty-three Fokker F28s, eighteen Fokker F27s and three Fokker F100s. Although the emphasis lies on the primary and secondary domestic network with over one hundred points served, some international routes to Malaysia and Australia are part of Merpati's schedule, too.

Opposite Here you see PK-GRK, one of Merpati's F27-500s, still in the old livery with simple 'Merpati' titles on the tail and 'Nusantara Airlines' lettering on the grey underside, that is separated from the white top of the fuselage by a broad two-tone brown cheatline.
(Author's Collection)

Below Already wearing the airline's current new colour scheme, Fokker F27-600, PK-MFD, is seen here. Meanwhile this aircraft has been sold, and the F27-fleet is standardized to the 500 version with a 56-seat configuration. The carrier's ICAO call sign is 'MERPATI'.
(Author's Collection)

MOUNT COOK AIRLINE (NM/NZM)   New Zealand

Mount Cook Airline is New Zealand's second largest airline and by far the oldest. Its roots trace back to August 1920, when Mount Cook's air transport operation was formed at Timaru as 'New Zealand Aero Transport Company' by Rodolph Wigley. On 13 January 1921, the first flight was made in a DH9A from Invercargill to Stewart Island. A few years later the airline went into liquidation, but in 1937 Rodolph Wigley again founded 'his' airline under the name 'Queenstown-Mount Cook Airways Ltd' using a Waco bi-plane on pleasure and charter flights. In 1954 the company obtained the licence to run a service from Christchurch to Mount Cook and Queenstown, but it took another seven years until the inaugural scheduled flight started on 6 November 1961, with the Douglas DC-3, ZK-AOD, along the Christchurch-Queenstown route. In 1968 the first Hawker Siddeley HS748 joined the fleet, and this type has been the fleet's backbone ever since. Christchurch is Mount Cook's headquarters, where nowadays a mixed fleet of Cessna 185 Skywagons, Pilatus Turbo-Porters, Piper PA-31 Navajos, Britten Norman BN-2A Islanders, DHC 6 Twin Otters, HS 748s and Fokker F27s is maintained and currently fourteen destinations are served. The airline is a division of the diversified travel and transport company 'The Mount Cook Group Ltd.', a fully-owned subsidiary of Air New Zealand. Apart from scheduled and charter passenger services, Mount Cook Airline is also engaged in scenic airtours and ski-flights with the Cessna Skywagon fleet based at Mount Cook Airport. This fleet is equipped with wheel-skis for flight-sightseeing around Milford Sound and Franz Josef Glacier. It is remarkable that the first skiplane flights were already carried out in September 1955, using an Auster Aiglet with 'self-made' skis attached to the undercarriage. Later, the Cessna 180 and 185 superseded the Austers. Based on the southern island, an agricultural division of Mount Cook Airline was doing cropdusting work with Fletcher FU24 planes. The origins of this division trace back to Central Aviation Ltd that had been integrated in April 1975. Due to the decline of the farming economy, the company was forced to 'mothball' agricultural flying activities in late 1986. In July 1987 the airline leased one Fokker F27 (ZK-DCB) from the New Zealand Ministry of Transport. The Fokker F27 was sold to Air UK in November 1991. Two months later another Fokker F27, ZK-BXF, was leased from Air New Zealand via Jetlease Inc., and operates on all Mount Cook Airline scheduled service routes as stand-by aircraft, equipped with a quite 'luxurious' 40-seat configuration. For its route from Christchurch to Rotorua, Mount Cook Air uses a hush-kitted Boeing B-737-200 leased from Air New Zealand since October 1992. Depicted at Christchurch Airport, you can here see Fokker F27-200, ZK-DCB. The airline's international call sign is 'MOUNTCOOK'. *(Author"s Collection)*

NAKA NIHON AIRLINE SERVICE (NAK)   Japan

The mother-holding Naka Nihon Air Service Co. Ltd was already established in 1953, under the name 'Naka Nihon Koku' at Nagoya. It operates extensive taxi, charter and contract passenger and cargo flights from its home base at Nagoya, with a fleet of Cessnas of various models and a large helicopter fleet, consisting of Bell 212s, Jet Rangers, Long Rangers, Big Lifters, Aérospaciale Lamas, Ecureuils, Dauphins, Super Pumas and Fuji-Bell 204s. In August 1988 the airline founded Naka Nihon Airline Service (NAL) as a new Japanese regional commuter airline, also based at Nagoya. Both companies belong to the Meitetsu Group, a subsidiary of Nagoya Railway. All Nippon Airways holds a 20 per cent interest in Naka Nihon Airline Service. The airline intended to operate scheduled services from Nagoya to Nankishirahama and Tamaya from 1 April 1989 on, but a decision about the fleet was not taken. Naka Nihon Airline Service planned to introduce a commuter plane with about 50 seats, but it took some time for the company to finally decide to buy two Fokker F50s for the routes. The first aircraft was delivered in November 1990. A second Fokker F50 was ordered in August 1991 and delivered exactly one year later. Both aircraft are leased from Meitetsu Sogo Kigyo and are equipped with a 'narrow' 56-seat configuration. The livery of Naka Nihon Airline Service is quite simple: the F50s sport a dark undercarriage, a white fuselage and deep red tail colours. The red tone continues on top of the fuselage and broadens towards the cockpit; the nose and the front wheel flaps are red as well. The company's logo is a white stylized seagull seen on the fin. Black 'NAL' lettering is applied beneath the cockpit. Here you see the airline's second Fokker 50, PH-EXX (today re-registered as JA8889), depicted during a test flight at Amsterdam, prior to delivery. *(Author's Collection)*

NLM (HN/NLM)

Netherlands

NLM, the acronym for 'Nederlandse Luchtvaart Maatschappij', was founded in 1966 and began operating scheduled flights on 29 August 1966, using two Fokker F27 Troopships leased from the Royal Dutch Air Force. Three weeks later, the airline was officially registered with the Chamber of Commerce in Haarlem, as a full subsidiary of KLM Royal Dutch Airlines, the Dutch flag-carrier. The initial network included six domestic destinations, served on twenty weekly flights: Amsterdam, Rotterdam, Eindhoven, Groningen, Maastricht and Enschede. In 1974 these feeder operations were expanded and the first international flight operations started from the airline's home base at Amsterdam. On 1 April 1974 the first scheduled international flight from Eindhoven took a NLM Fokker F27 to Hamburg. For all the company's life, the Fokker F27 has been the fleet's backbone. Fourteen units have been operated altogether during the decades, transporting over 12.5 million passengers. The aircraft could easily be converted and so it was possible to use it for passenger transportation during the day and parcel and cargo flights at night. To emphasize the international character of its European network, the famous name 'City Hopper' was added in 1977. One year later the first of five Fokker F28-4000 jets joined the fleet, to be mainly used on international services from Amsterdam

and Rotterdam. Prime destinations were Belfast, Birmingham, Brussels, Düsseldorf, Hamburg, Jersey, London and Stuttgart. Additionally, the aircraft were used on charter contracts and on several KLM flights. On 1 April 1991, KLM merged its two regional subsidiaries NLM and Netherlines under the new name 'KLM City Hopper' and modernized the fleet. Fokker F50s replaced the old F27s, and ten weeks later, the F27-good-bye flight took place between Eindhoven and Amsterdam. The aircraft still had NLM livery. After the withdrawal, the Fokker F27s were sold to Myanma Airways in December 1991.

Fokker F27-200, PH-KFG *Koos Abspoel*, is depicted here during take-off at Amsterdam's Schiphol Airport for flight HN463 to Eindhoven on 24 October 1989. The traditional colour scheme consists of a twin-cheatline in a two-tone blue, the darker of which runs along at window level, the brighter above, both bending and broadening into the tail. 'NLM City Hopper' titles are integrated in the upper line over the front door and big 'City Hopper' lettering is diagonally displayed in the fin. NLM's ICAO call sign was 'CITY'.
(W. Kathe)

NORCANAIR (NT/NKA) Canada

Norcanair is a regional Canadian carrier based at Saskatoon/Saskatchewan. Its history traces back to the year 1965, when it was founded in January. Two months later Norcanair took over the traditional Saskair, that had originally been formed in 1947 as 'Saskatchewan Government Airways'. In the 1970s a colourfully mixed fleet of Cessna Skywagons, de Havilland DHC2 Beavers, DHC3 Otters, DHC6 Twin Otters, Piper PA-23 Aztecs, PA-31 Navajos, Douglas DC-3s, Consolidated Cansos, Bristol 170 freighters and Fairchild F-27A/Js was maintained. Scheduled passenger flights operated over expanded routes in Alberta and Saskatchewan. Charter operations were made throughout Canada and the USA. The airline became a division of High Line Airways in 1983. In October 1984 seven Fokker F28s were ordered to be operated on the scheduled services from Saskatoon to Edmonton, Minneapolis and Calgary. During the 1980s Convair CV640 and Beechcraft King Air joined the fleet and the number of Fairchild F-27s was reduced.

Main routes were Regina-Saskatoon-Prince Albert, North Battleford-Saskatoon, Regina-Saskatoon-Lloydminster-Edmonton and La Ronge-Uranium City-Stony Rapids. In April 1987, Norcanair was taken over by Time Air (Alberta), an airline which has been closely associated with Canadian International (46 per cent). Gradually the aircraft were painted in Canadian Airlines International colours and integration was finished on 1 January 1988. Nevertheless, Norcanair survived as a name behind stage and became reactivated in 1990. Today, the airline's small fleet consists of one Beechcraft King Air 90, one Convair CV640 and one Fairchild F-27J. This plane, C-GCRA, is here seen in full Norcanair livery in summer 1986. The aircraft are coloured in brightest blue except for a dark blue cheatline and similarly coloured 'Norcanair' titles behind the cockpit. The airline's traditional tail logo represents a compass-needle. The ICAO call sign is 'NORCANAIR'.
(Author's Collection)

NORDAIR (ND/NDR)   Canada

Nordair was one of the oldest independent Canadian regional
airlines when it merged into Canadian Airlines in 1987. The airline
had originally been founded in 1947 under the name 'Boreal
Airways.' In 1953 Mont Laurier Aviation was acquired and four years
later the airline changed its name to 'Nordair'. Activities in Arctic
Canada and around the Hudson Bay region were intensified by
absorbing Wheeler Airlines in 1960, and in 1971 the first
international services from Toronto, Montreal and Ottawa to
Pittsburgh started. In early 1979 the Toronto-Winnipeg route was
taken over from Transair. In addition to the scheduled services
throughout Quebec, Ontario, Manitoba and N.W.T., cargo and
passenger charter operations were undertaken. Nordair provided
vital air transportation between southern Canada and remote places
in the Arctic, but also holiday flights to Florida, organized by
Treasure Tours, a subsidiary of Nordair. From time to time
additional contract services were carried out for the Canadian
government and the United States Air Force. In 1985 ownership
shifted from Air Canada, which had held an 86.4 per cent interest
before, to CP Air. Nevertheless, Nordair still operated a fleet of five
FH-227s, thirteen Boeing B-737-200s and two Lockheed Electras
used for ice reconnaissance in its own colours. The last colour
scheme, unveiled in 1983, consisted of two blue cheatlines, one
bright blue line over the windows and a darker and smaller stripe
below. The cockpit region was painted like an egg-shaped yellow
oval reaching the top between the first door and the wing. As a fin-
logo a three-dimensional crystal-like symbolic figure appeared,
consisting of five full or half-rhombs in the two blue tones of the
fuselage lines. 'NORDAIR' titles were applied in dark blue capital
letters behind the front door. In summer 1987 Nordair was
integrated into Canadian International and the aircraft were painted
in Canadian International colours. Nordair Metro and Quebecair
merged and operated under the name 'Inter Canadian' in full
Canadian livery. Here you can see C-GNDH, a Fairchild FH-227B, in
early 1988. *(Author's Collection)*

NOROESTE (5T/ANW)　　　　Mexico

Noroeste was formed in 1988, when the Mexican government decided to support new regional airlines that should operate in certain, limited geographical areas of the 'Estados Unidos Mexicanos' with turboprops equipped with 40-50 seats. The airline's full name is 'Aviacion del Noroeste, SA de CV' with its home base at Hermosillo. In the beginning, Noroeste leased two 44-seat Fairchild F-27s from the French regional carrier Air Service Nantes. Operations started in October 1988. One of the F-27s was later on occasionally sub-leased to Aviacsa for operations from Tuxtla-Guiterrez. In July 1989 Noroeste placed an order for four CASA CN.235 Nurtanios, but they were not delivered. In May 1990 the Fairchild F-27 F-GHXA crashed into a hill on the approach to Tuxtla-Guiterrez. It had been on a scheduled flight for Aviacsa de Chiapas. Noroeste, the 'Linea del Progreso', mainly links Hermosillo (Sonora) with cities in southern USA and northwestern Mexico. For its domestic services and for the routes to San Diego and Los Angeles in California and Tucson and Phoenix in Arizona, the airline ordered two ATR 42s for delivery in late 1990. The two remaining Fairchild F-27s were replaced by ATR 42s and Boeing B-737-500s (leased from GPA) in early 1992 and late 1993. At that time the last F-27 was finally withdrawn from use. In November 1992 Noroeste gave up all its scheduled operations and the ATR 42s only operated for Taesa to various places on Yucatan. Taesa planned to take over Noroeste completely. Two Fokker F50s, ordered but never taken over by Noroeste, were directly delivered to Rio Sul, Brazil. Depicted in August 1989, Fairchild F-27J, F-GHXA, is seen here. The simple livery consists of a thin green and blue line below window level and on the engine, a blue 'N' on the tail and blue 'Noroeste' titles between wing and cockpit. The airline's ICAO call sign is 'AVINOR'. *(Author's Collection)*

NORTHWEST AIRLINES (NW/NWA)

United States of America

Northwest Airlines has often been called the 'silent giant' among US carriers, because of the airline's conservative and traditional management. In fact, Northwest is the second oldest airline in the USA and was founded on 1 August 1926, by some businessmen at the 'twin-city' Minneapolis and St. Paul, still being the company's operational base. During the first year contracts to transport mail were carried out and 106 passengers joined the airline on its sole route from Minneapolis to Chicago. When the Pacific services were initiated in 1947, Northwest Airways changed its name to 'Northwest Orient'. On 15 July 1947 a DC-4 took-off from Anchorage to operate the first scheduled flight via Tokyo, Seoul and Shanghai to Manila. As the DC-4 became too small, Boeing B-377 Stratocruisers and Douglas DC-6s were purchased for these routes. After a period of experimentation with various types of aircraft, Northwest Orient began standardizing its fleet to an all-Boeing affair in 1962. During the decades Boeing B-720, B-707, B-727, B-747 and B-757 of various series joined the fleet. One exception, however, was the decision to order nineteen Douglas DC-10-40 series, especially designed for Northwest's purposes and delivered between 1972 and 1974. When United Airlines took over Pan Am's Pacific division in February 1986, Northwest and United became direct competitors. As United had by far the better domestic network, Northwest was forced to react: the airline took over Republic Airlines which has been fully integrated into the Northwest fleet (DC-9s, CV580s and Boeing

B-727s) thereafter. Like the other main US airlines Northwest has a subdivision for regional flights where four commuter airlines are linked under the name 'Northwest Airlink'. The Fokker F27 is operated by Mesaba Airlines based at Minneapolis. The company's network includes destinations in Minnesota, North & South Dakota, Nebraska and Iowa. In October 1993 the airline decided to withdraw the remaining nine Fokker F27s from use and to replace them with Dash 8s. Today, Northwest maintains an amazingly heterogenous fleet of about 400 aircraft, comprising Airbus A320s, Boeing B-727s, B-747-100/200 and 400 series, B-757s, Douglas DC-9-10/30/40 and 50 series, Douglas MD-80s and DC-10-30/40 series. Northwest Airlink (Express Air, Mesaba Air, Northeast Express and Precision Air) operates Beechcraft 99s, Swearingen Metro IIIs, Dornier Do228s, DHC Dash 8s, Fokker F27s, Saab SF340A/Bs and BAe Jetstream 31 commuters, each in full Northwest colours. Until the present day the focal points of operation are the northwest of the USA and the Pacific network.

Here you see the Fokker F27-500 N284MA, formerly Air New South Wales/Australia, in a hybrid colour scheme, the fuselage is all white with new 'Northwest Airlink' titles, the tail is still coloured in traditional pure red. Tiny black 'Mesaba' stickers can be identified above the registration. Northwest's ICAO call sign is 'NORTH-WEST', Mesaba's ICAO sign is 'MESABA'. *(W. Kathe)*

RATIOFLUG (WR/RAT)　　　　Germany

Ratioflug GmbH was founded in 1982 starting as an air-taxi company with Piper PA-31 Navajo and Cessna 414/421 aircraft. In 1986 a Cessna 404 and a 14-seat Swearingen Merlin IV joined the fleet; further Cessna 404/414s and Swearingen Merlin/Metros followed in the late 1980s. In July 1988 the first Fokker F27-400 was taken over. It has a 44-seat configuration and is easily convertible to serve as a freighter with a cargo capacity of 5500 kg. On 1 January 1990, Ratioflug became 100 per cent owned by Ratioflug Holding. Today the airline maintains a fleet of one Cessna 404, one Dornier Do228, one Learjet 34A, two Learjet 55s and four Fokker F27-600s. Today, air-taxi operations are still an important part of the airline's activities. Ratioflug created a new image in the early 1990s to increase attractivity of the service offered to business people. Flights are comfortable, individual and the Learjets are luxuriously equipped. As Frankfurt is Ratioflug's home-base, the airline has the exceptional permission to operate flights during the night except for a period between 1.00 a.m. and 4.00 a.m., when no landings are allowed. The Fokker F27s are mainly used as freighters. Scheduled cargo flight contracts exist for the routes from Cologne to Basle and from Cologne to Paris-Orly. A daily cargo flight links Frankfurt with Bergamo. The aircraft's colour schemes differ: the Dornier Do228 is operated in all-white. The Learjets are basically white as well, but thin black and brown lines run diagonally over the fuselage from nose to tail, underlining the plane's elegant design. The Fokker F27s sports two cheatlines, with a broader blue line at window level and a narrow golden-brown line above. Blue 'Ratioflug' titles are applied below. The tail usually remains white. An unconventional 'triple r' tail-logo can here be seen on Fokker F27-600, D-ADEP, depicted on the tarmac at Munich-Riem Airport on 30 March 1992. Ratioflug's ICAO call sign is 'BATMAN'. *(W. Kathe)*

RIO SUL (SL/RSL)   Brazil

Established as a commuter airline on 24 August, 1976, Rio Sul began operations two weeks later on the route from Porto Alegre to Pelotas. Rio Sul, or giving in its full title, 'Rio-Sul Servicios Aereos Regionais SA', is a subsidiary of the Brazilian national carrier VARIG (Viacao Aerea Rio-Grandense), which has a 51.67 per cent holding in Rio Sul. Since 1981 the company reported operational profits and gradually expanded. In 1985, Rio Sul operated a fleet of six Embraer 110P Bandeirantes and six Fokker F27s from its home-base at Rio de Janeiro-Santos Dumont Airport. The airline mainly concentrates on regional services in the seven southeastern states of Brazil: Espirito Santo, Minas Gerais, Parana, Rio de Janeiro, Rio Grande do Sul, Santa Catarina and São Paolo. Today a dense network of routes is covered from the main hubs at Curitiba, Porto Alegre, Rio de Janeiro-Santos Dumont and São Paolo-Congonhas and over 35 places are served. The airline staff, pilots and crew members are usually trained by the company itself. In October 1986 Rio Sul ordered the first two Embraer 120 Brasilias for delivery in late 1987 and took options on another five which were converted into orders in autumn 1988. In January 1990 four Fokker F27s were sold to Pakistan International; at the same time Rio Sul began a shuttle service on the famous 'Ponte Aerea' between Rio de Janeiro and São Paolo, with six daily flights. The airline uses Embraer 120 Brasilias for this service, competing with VARIG and TAM shuttle flights. In August 1992 Rio Sul got its first two Fokker F50s; these had originally been ordered but never taken over by Noroeste, Mexico. Two F27s were returned to Fokker in exchange. For the flights from São Paolo and Rio to Brasilia, Rio Sul purchased two Boeing B-737-500s, the company's first jets, which were delivered in October and December 1992. Depicted here in August 1993, is PT-SLR, one of Rio Sul's brand new Fokker F50s, on its delivery flight. The aircraft displays the airline's new colour scheme, featuring the 'modern' white fuselage with 'Rio-Sul' in blue, thick script and the traditional fin-logo in a three-tone blue with three additional diagonal stripes in the same tones. The airline's ICAO call sign is 'RIOSUL'. (Author's Collection)

ROYAL AIR INTER (RN/RAI)   Morocco

In the late 1960s the extent of air traffic increased also in Morocco and a demand for domestic flights arose. Consequently, a domestic airline was founded by the state of Morocco and Royal Air Maroc in 1970. The new airline — 'Royal Air Inter' — had an initial capital of 8 million Dirham. The government owned 57.5 per cent of the airline, the residual 42.5 per cent were held by Royal Air Maroc. The airline operated on a quite dense network, but some of the smaller places were either served once a week or as required. Cities served in Morocco were Al Hoceima, Agadir, Rabat, Casablanca, Tanger, Tetouan, Marrakech, Fes, Ouzazate and Oujda; additionally some places in the politically controversial West-Sahara were served, like Tantan, Dakhla, Smara, Er Rachida and La'youn. The only international services operated by Royal Air Inter were scheduled flights linking Casablanca, Agadir and La'youn to Las Palmas/ Canary Islands. The fleet of Royal Air Inter consisted of two Fokker F27 turboprops from its early days in 1970 until the end. Both aircraft belonged to the Mk600 series and were equipped with 40 seats. Their home base was Casablanca. In September 1988 Royal Air Maroc ordered three ATR42s to replace Royal Air Inter's F27s. The ATR 42s were delivered in April and May 1989 and were painted up in full Royal Air Maroc colours. Royal Air Inter became finally integrated into Royal Air Maroc in August 1989 and the two Fokker F27s were sold to the Danish Starair. The Fokker F27 CN-CDA is seen here on one of its scheduled flights at Las Palmas in December 1987. The carrier's ICAO call sign was 'ROMEO NOVEMBER'.
(W. Kathe)

SAS-SCANDINAVIAN AIRLINES
(SK/SAS)

Denmark, Norway, Sweden

Scandinavian Airlines is in fact the world's first multi-national carrier, formed on 1 August 1946, when the three Scandinavian airlines DDL (Det Danske Luftfartselskab A/S), DNL (Det Norske Luftfartselskab A/S) and ABA (AB Aerotransport) fused and formed SAS-Scandinavian Airlines System. Initially the idea was to establish common transatlantic flights, but later co-operation should be extended to all air-services. The owners agreed upon a 2 (DDL):2 (DNL):3 (ABA = SILA) proportion, the airline had six independent directors, and all staff was to be employed by the syndicate. The fleet, however, was still operated by the national carriers. The three airlines have been 50 per cent state and 50 per cent privately-owned, since then. In the 1950s a large fleet of Douglas DC-3s, DC-4s, DC-6s, DC-7s, Saab Scandias and Convair CV440s was maintained. SAS was the first airline to operate the SE210 Caravelle on 26 April, 1959 and two years later the first Douglas DC-8 joined the fleet for long-haul flights. Boeing B-747s, Convair CV990s, A300s, Douglas DC-10s and DC-9s all series, MD-80s and Boeing B-767-200/300s were operated during the years, but only the latter three types are still in service today. The Danish domestic network has mainly been operated under the name Danair, using SAS (Douglas

DC-9s), Maersk Air (Boeing B-737s, Dash 7s, now Fokker F50s) and Cimber Air (Nord ND 262) aircraft, but in 1984 SAS commuter services were reactivated by buying a couple of Fokker F27s. The F50-fleet, which began to replace the F27, is operated under the name 'Scandinavian Commuter', an SAS subsidiary, founded in 1988. It consists of two divisions, the Tromsoe-based 'Norlink' for domestic services in Norway, and the Copenhagen-based 'Eurolink' for regional flights from Copenhagen to Sweden and between South Scandinavia and places in Europe. Seen here at Prague-Ruzyne Airport on 6 April 1992, Scandinavian Commuter's F50, OY-KAH *Bjoern Viking*, displays the airline's current livery. A white overall fuselage shows a front-striped rhombus of the three national colours. Small black 'Scandinavian Commuter' titles appear behind. Instead of the usual 'SAS' tail titles, the three national flags and diagonally-applied 'Eurolink' characters can be seen on the fin. In late 1992 Linjeflyg, the main domestic competitor, was taken over and the fleet (Fokker F28s, Boeing B-737-300 and -500s) integrated. These ex-Linjeflyg aircraft, however, did not meet the SAS fleet plan and thus most were gradually sold during 1994. The airline's ICAO call sign is 'SCANDINAVIAN'. *(W. Kathe)*

SCHREINER AIRWAYS (AW/SCH)   Netherlands

Schreiner Airways, B.V. can trace its history back nearly fifty years. It was originally formed in 1945 to represent aircraft manufacturers. Own transport operations then started in 1959. Today international and domestic contract and charter services are operated. Schreiner Airways is also engaged in flight training. The airline is a subsidiary of Schreiner Aviation Group B.V., with KLM, the Dutch national carrier, as a minority shareholder. Scores of joint ventures have been established overseas, mainly in Angola, Argentina, Australia, Bolivia, Chile, India, Indonesia, Malaysia, Nigeria, Phillippines, Qatar, Thailand and United Arab Emirates. The airline's home base and maintenance centre is Maastricht, where a large fleet of helicopters and aircraft of various types, Pipers, Dash 8s and Fokker F27s is maintained. Schreiner's F27s operations began in May 1986 with a Fokker F27-400 purchased for cargo flights from Maastricht (PH-SFA, ex N710A, ARAMCO). At the same time, the airline planned to introduce scheduled passenger flights from Maastricht to Groningen, Eindhoven and some European destinations like Paris, Stuttgart and London which were, however, never run. In August 1986 Schreiner Airways founded City Air Limburg as a

subsidiary for passenger charter flights from Maastricht Airport, using two Schreiner Fokker F27s. Two more Fokker F27s were operated for XP Parcel System, until this company was sold to TNT. Consequently both Fokker F27s were sold to Malmö Aviation who operated contracts for TNT. In August 1989 Schreiner Airways bought an Air Gabon Lockheed L100.30 Hercules that had flown for KLM, mainly on cargo flights between Amsterdam, Stockholm and Gothenburg. The freighter was replaced by an ex-KLM A310 in December 1990. In April 1990 three Fokker F27s were sold to BP-British Petroleum for global survey flights and a few weeks later the first Dash 8 was delivered to Schreiner Airways, flying for Mobil Oil in West Africa. Two more Dash 8s were purchased in October 1990 and wet-leased to Sabena (in full such colours) for three years to serve between Brussels, Marseille, Lyon and Bordeaux. Depicted here at Maastricht-Zuid Limburg Airport in May 1986, you see the first Fokker F27-400, PH-SFA, after delivery. The plane was operated in a simple livery with an orange cheatline and a white tail, not sporting Schreiner's usual triple-S logo. The airline's ICAO call sign is 'SCHREINER'. *(W. Kathe)*

SEMPATI AIR (SG/SSR)   Indonesia

Sempati Air is one of the early Indonesian private airlines, founded on 16 December 1968 under the name 'Sempati Air Transport'. In the beginning the airline operated charter contracts for oil companies like Stanvac and Caltex Indonesia with Douglas DC-3 (or C-47) aircraft. In May 1972 the first Fokker F27-200 joined the fleet and in 1974 another Fokker F27 (600 series) was bought from Garuda (PK-JFF), which unfortunately crashed during a test-flight at Surabaya-Juanda on 5 June 1991. Between 1977 and 1985 four more Fokker F27s were leased and later bought from Danish Aero Lease and Aviona Leasing. All F27s are equipped with 44 Y-class seats. Between 1975 and 1978 the airline operated international scheduled flights from Jakarta and Denpasar to Tokyo with a leased Boeing B-707; these services had to be given up, however, after the licence was suspended by the Indonesian Government, because the state-owned airline Garuda took over the route. In 1989 Sempati Air Transport reorganized, the company's name was changed into 'Sempati Air' and more and more scheduled services were introduced covering Sumatra and the surrounding islands. The shareholders changed and today 40 per cent are held by Pt. Tri

Usaha Bhakti, 35 per cent by Pt. Nusamba and 25 per cent by Pt. Humpuss. Private Indonesian companies were not allowed to operate jets until the early 1990s. Sempati Air got the exceptional permission to operate jets in June 1990 and the airline leased seven Fokker F100s from GPA, which were originally ordered by Pan Am/Braniff. They operate on some main Indonesian routes from Jakarta to Denpasar, Ujungpandang, Medan, Batam, Balikpapan and Surabaya. In October 1992 Sempati took over the first Boeing B-737-200 from All Nippon Airlines. Today Sempati Air operates a fleet of five Fokker F27s, seven Fokker 100s, six Boeing B737-200s and three Airbus A300B4s. The Airbus is mainly used on the airline's new international services from Jakarta to Perth, Singapore, Penang, Kuala Lumpur and Taipeh and further A300s are planned to be added. In July 1993 Sempati ordered the new Fokker F70, a shorter version of the Fokker F100, as launch customer. Ten units will be delivered after 1995. Here PK-JFI is depicted in the airline's old livery. Sempati Air's ICAO call sign is 'SPIROW'.
(Author's Collection)

STAR AIR (DQ/SRR)   Denmark

In September 1987, A.P. Möller Group, the owner of Maersk Air, founded Star Air as a 100 per cent subsidiary of Maersk Air. The new company leased the three Alkair Fokker F27s to use them on cargo and passenger charter flights. The aircraft operated in all white colours for a short time, before they were painted in a blue colour scheme, very similar to the Maersk Air livery. The whole fin and roof of the fuselage shine in bright blue colours, the windowline is white and the aircraft display a black-blue underside with integrated white 'Star Air' titles in small lettering. Star Air's tail logo is a white star framed by a white rectangular line. A heavy loss for the airline was the crash of Fokker F27-600, OY-APE, on 26 May 1988 on the final approach to Hannover, Germany. The aircraft was completely destroyed and the two crew members were killed. The Fokker had operated a scheduled cargo-flight for TNT (Australia) from Billund (Denmark) via Hannover to Nürnberg. The official reason for the crash was a moving load that made the F27 loose balance during the final approach. The Fokker F27 was replaced by another plane of the same type which was purchased from Air UK. One Fokker F27 (OY-SRB) was leased to Northwest Airlink in June 1989 and the two ex-Royal Air Inter Fokker F27s were bought instead. In October 1989 a Fokker F27 was operated on behalf of the Irish company IONA National Airways for Fedex on parcel flights. Another F27 was sold to Conair Canada and replaced the F27 that had crashed near Arles in France, two months before. Today, Star Air operates four Fokker F27-600s, two of them are equipped with 44 seats, two are freighters. Besides its current Fokker F27 fleet, Star Air began operating two Boeing B-727-100 freighters with Danish registration for UPS, in November 1993. They are kept busy with scheduled night services between Cologne, Bergamo and Rome, to Zaragoza and Porto. Seen here at Munich-Riem Airport on 31 March 1988, Fokker F27-600, OY-APE, is depicted about two months before it crashed at Hannover. Star Air's ICAO call sign is 'WHITESTAR'. *(W. Kathe)*

SUDAN AIRWAYS (SD/SUD)   Sudan

The fully state-owned Sudanese flag-carrier was founded in 1946 and began flight activities one year later. In July 1947 the routes from Khartoum to Port Sudan, Juba and Asmara were operated using a de Havilland Dove. Today sixteen domestic locations are served, main operations running between Khartoum and El Obeid, Dongola, Juba and Port Sudan. International destinations are Addis Ababa, Abu Dhabi, Cairo, Damascus, Doha, Jeddah, N'Djamena, Kano, Nairobi, Rijadh, Sharjah and Sanaa; Athens, Rome, Frankfurt and London are served in Europe. For a long time Boeing B-707s were used on the European flights, but they are refused landing permission today, not being hush-kitted. Due to the shooting down of a Sudan Airways Fokker F27 in summer 1986, when all the passengers were killed, the airline decided to stop all scheduled and aid-operations to South Sudan. In February 1987 Sudan Airways changed some of its international services to Lockheed Tristar for a short time. The aircraft was leased from Royal Jordanian Airlines, which supported Sudan Air technically. The routes served were Khartoum-Cairo-Athens-London and Khartoum-Cairo-Rome-Frankfurt-London. For a short time in summer 1988 a Nationair DC-8 was leased that operated on some international routes but never had full Sudan Airways livery. After the aircraft had been returned, the European services were operated by Boeing B-737-200s before they were suspended for some time. To replace the remaining Fokker F27s, Sudan Airways ordered four Fokker F50s, but only two were delivered. In the meantime three more Fokker F27s had to be leased. Two of them were originally ordered by Fuerza Aerea Guatemalteca, operated in the concerning colour scheme but the lease ended in September 1989, when the first Fokker F50 was delivered. The Fuerza Aerea Guatemalteca-coloured Fokker F27 ST-ALF was returned to Fokker and revised at Maastricht. This aircraft is depicted here on the tarmac of Maastricht-Zuid Limburg Airport in September 1989. In December 1990 Sudan Airways wet-leased one Airbus A310-300 from Royal Jordanian which was, however, only in service for a few weeks and then stored at Maastricht due to the escalation of the Gulf crisis. In 1992 a second A310, which is still in service, joined the fleet and the first A320 was delivered just recently. The airline's ICAO call sign is 'SUDANAIR'. *(W. Kathe)*

SUNSHINE AVIATION (OC/SHS)   Switzerland

Sunshine Aviation was formed in 1985 with six employees and two aircraft, one Piper PA-31 Navajo and one Piper PA-42 Cheyenne, as an air-taxi company based at Lugano in the Swiss county Ticino. In July 1986 a 17-seat Dornier Do 228 was purchased and a licence to operate scheduled services was applied for. In April 1987, Sunshine Aviation was given the certificate of the Swiss Aviation Administration and began operating charter services between its home base Lugano and places in Italy using the Do 228. The colour scheme introduced, consisted of a stylized half sun with two red central and one yellow outer circle and a small red airplane flying into the sun plus large red Sunshine titles on a white fuselage. The tail carried the obligatory small Swiss cross (white on red). In early summer 1988, Sunshine Aviation bought two Fokker F27s from Finnair (ex OH-LKA and LKC). Balair overhauled the Fokkers at Basle, because they had been stored for some time and painted them in full Sunshine colours. The first commercial flight took-off from Zürich bound for Hyères on 19 January 1989. In the beginning the F27s were used for charter services from various Swiss airports. Starting on 25 September 1989, the Fokker F27 HB-ISH regularly operated between Lugano (Switzerland), Rome-Fiumicino and Florence (Italy) by order of Transavio. On weekends, charter flights were carried out, mainly on the Basle — Olbia (Sardinia) route. As the planes were still maintained by Balair, Sunshine shifted its technical base from Lugano to Basle as well. In early 1989 the Dornier Do 228 HB-LPC was leased to Arcus Air, Mannheim for a scheduled service between Mannheim and Hamburg, that only ran for some weeks and one Fokker F27 was leased to the United Nations for a short period. In April 1989 Sunshine ordered one Dornier Do 328 for delivery in 1993. In late 1993 the two Fokker F27s, however, were stored at Basle and the Do 228 was leased to Air Engiadina, after the lease to Transavio was finished because the municipal council withheld permission for F27 operations into Lugano due to noise restrictions. In December 1993 the airline merged with Air Engiadina.

HB-ISG, one of Sunshine's Fokker F27-200s is depicted here on approach to Munich-Riem Airport on 19 October 1989. The airline's ICAO call sign was 'SUNSHINE'. *(W. Kathe)*

TAM — TRANSPORTES AÉREOS REGIONAIS (KK/TAM)
Brazil

TAM's history dates back to January 1961, when Taxi Aereo Marilia, the first airline of the actual TAM group, was formed. In May 1976 Taxi Aereo Marilia and VASP established TAM as a regional airline for the São Paulo region, starting with an Embraer 110 Bandeirante. The airline's first flight took off at São Paulo on 12 July 1976, operating to Ourinhos and Maringa. Today the TAM group consists of four subdivisions, TAM-Airlines, Taxi Aereo Marilia, TAM-Executive Jets and Brazil Central. The airline is controlled by private interests, with Taxi Aereo Marilia holding a majority share. Until 1992 TAM was associated with VASP. The airline is based at São Paulo-Congonhas and is the largest Brazilian regional carrier, with 1.2 million passengers transported in 1993. TAM concentrates on the South of Brazil around São Paulo, which is the most industrialized area in the whole country, mainly offering scheduled services throughout the states of Mato Grosso, Minas Gerais, Parana, Rio de Janeiro, São Paulo and to Brasilia. In September 1989 TAM started operating on the 'Ponte Aerea' between Rio de Janeiro (Santos Dumont) and São Paulo (Congonhas), a service that had been a monopoly of the V.A.R.I.G. Lockheed L-188 Electras for a very long time. TAM first used Fokker F27s and Embraer 110 Bandeirantes for the shuttle. In June 1990 TAM bought two Fokker F100s from GPA and optioned on another two, which replaced the F27s on the Ponte Aerea in November 1992. Today a fleet of thirteen F100s and seven Fokker F27s is maintained and the combined network of TAM and Brazil Central (Cessna Caravans, E110 Bandeirantes and Fokker F27s) includes 53 Brazilian cities and international flights to Asuncion/Paraguay. Depicted here during flight, you see Fokker F27-500, PT-LAL. The type was introduced in January 1980. Today a 52-seat F27-500 series and the 44-seat F27-600 version are used for passenger flights between twelve Brazilian cities and on cargo and postal flights for the Brazilian Post Service during the night. The main F27 routes cover Belo Horizonte-Rio, São Paulo-Marilia, São Paulo-Aracatuba, Rio-San Jose de Rio Preto and Ribeirao Preto-Goiania-Brasilia. The airline's ICAO call sign is 'TAM'. *(TAM Brazil)*

TAT (ITAT)   France

TAT was established in 1968. At that time the abbreviation stood for 'Touraine Air Transport'. Scheduled flight operations commenced in 1970 from its operational base at Tours-St. Symphorien Airport. During the 1970s and 1980s various French commuter airlines were absorbed by TAT, such as Air Alpes, Air Alsace, Air Languedoc, Air Paris, Rousseau Aviation and Taxi Avia France. A fleet of Beechcraft 99s, Cessna 310s, and Cessna 150s had been maintained, when in the late 1970s Ozark's Fairchild FH-227B fleet was purchased and the first Fokker F28s joined the fleet. During the following years, TAT established a dense network of scheduled domestic services throughout France and Corsica, including some services operated on behalf of Air France and charter contracts. TAT's subsidiary TAT Export (IO/TTX) operated international charters and the scheduled service from Berlin to Saarbrücken, until Dan Air took over the route in 1984. Between 1981 and 1986 all Fokker F28 aircraft were leased out or operated for Air France in full Air France colours. A serious accident affected the airline on 4 March 1988, when FH-227 F-GCPS crashed near Paris-Orly on the final approach and all 22 passengers of the flight from Nancy were killed. In October 1988 TAT ordered 20 ATR 72s to replace the over twenty-year-old Fairchild FH-227 fleet. For leasing out parts of the

fleet, a leasing company was founded (50 per cent TAT, 10 per cent Aérospaciale and 40 per cent banks). In August 1989 Air France purchased 35 per cent of TAT and therefore the co-operation between both airlines was intensified. On 12 July 1991 the last official FH-227 flight was run from Lille to Paris-Orly. Seen here at the tarmac of Nuremberg Airport in December 1985, Fairchild FH-227B, F-GCPV, is depicted in the old all-yellow livery. In November 1992 British Airways purchased 49.9 per cent of TAT. Many European TAT services were offered under BA flight numbers and a couple of Fokkers, F28 and F100, were painted up in full British Airways colours. As a consequence Air France cancelled contracts with TAT, and in the summer schedule 1994 no TAT operations on behalf of Air France were left. Four hundred employees were dismissed and less profitable domestic routes given up. Today the airline operates a reduced fleet, of Beechcraft 200s, ATR 42/72s, Fokker F28s, F100s and Boeing B-737s in a new, different livery, introduced with the ATR 42 in 1990: the fuselage is all white with large 'TAT' — and small 'European Airlines' titles; the tail colours are still yellow with three blue waves resembling stylized birds. The airline's ICAO call sign is 'TAT'. *(W. Kathe)*

UNITED AIRLINES (UA/UAL) United States of America

The world's second largest airline of today has a long history that goes back to 1926 and to four independent airlines: Boeing Air Transport, starting operations between San Francisco and Chicago in July 1987; National Air Transport, commencing scheduled flights from Chicago to Kansas City and Dallas in May 1926; Pacific Air Transport going into business with scheduled operations on the Seattle-Los Angeles route in September 1926, and finally Varney Air Lines, carrying out mail services between Boise, Elko and Pasco. In 1929 Boeing and Pacific Air Transport were linked under the 'United Aircraft and Transport Corporation' holding. When the two other airlines joined the corporation in 1930, the four consolidated under the name 'United Airlines' in July 1931. This name has remained unchanged to today. With the absorption of Capital Airlines in 1961, United Airlines became the largest US carrier. The airline's main hub and administrative centre is Chicago; a second hub and a flight training centre has been established at Denver-Stapleton and the major maintenance facilities are located at San Francisco. In June 1985, United Airlines bought the car-rental company Hertz. Some months later, the airline took over both Pan Am's Pacific network and the Boeing B-747SP and Lockheed L1011 aircraft and thus made its first step to build up an international network. On 4 April 1991,

United took over all Pan Am flights to London using a mixture of Boeing B-747-100/SPs and B-767s. After the last DC-8s had been sold in 1992, United now operates a fleet of Boeing B-727-200s, B-737-200/300/500s, B-747-100/200/400/SPs, B-757s, B-767-200/300s, Airbus A320s and Douglas DC-10-10/30s, altogether over 400 aircraft. The new Boeing B-777 has been ordered for delivery in 1995. The commuter division 'United Express' was established in 1986, providing feeder services to United's main hubs and serving local and remote places. Today, the United Express Group consists of five airlines: Air Wisconsin, Atlantic Coast Airlines, Great Lake Airlines, Mesa Airlines and Westair Commuter Airlines. A fleet of Fokker F27s, Dash 8s, BAe ATPs, BAe 146s, BAe Jetstream 31/41s, Embraer 120 Brasilias, Shorts 360s and Beechcraft 1900 Airliners is maintained. In early 1993, United Airlines unveiled its new livery, a dark blue fuselage which resembles that of Canadian Airlines and USAir. The Fokker F27-500, N506AW, is here seen in late 1988. The fuselage displays full United Airlines colours and the UA Express tail logo consisting of three simple beams in orange, red and blue. Like the other F27s, it has been operated by Air Wisconsin, but is now out of service. United's ICAO call sign is 'UNITED'.
(Author's Collection)

VLM (V4/VLM)   Belgium

VLM — the acronym stands for 'Vlaamse Luchtvaart Maatschappij' — is a quite young airline. It was founded in March 1992 by Freddy van Gaever, a man who had always played a major role in Antwerp aviation. Many years before, he had also founded DAT — Delta Air Transport — and he owns FREVAG, a Belgian leasing company. The intention was to establish an independent commuter airline operating from the home base Antwerp, Belgium. First plans included scheduled services with Swearingen Metroliners from Antwerp to Munich, Hamburg and Paris, but they couldn't be realized at that time. In April 1993 VLM finally took over two Fokker F50s from former Busy Bee Norway, which had to sell its all-Fokker fleet after having suspended operations. Both F50s are leased-in from Prime Aviation A/S and are used on scheduled flights between

Antwerp and London City Airport was well as for charter operations and taxi flights throughout Europe. A third Fokker F50 was taken over from BASE Air, Eindhoven in December 1993 to extend charter operations. All aircraft have a 50-seat one-class configuration. The livery of VLM is a hybrid mixture: along the window-line runs a dark yellow cheatline framed by two narrow brown streaks. They all taper towards the front and curve downwards beneath the fin to meet the cheatlines of the opposite side. This basic colour scheme is the unchanged Busy Bee livery. On the white fin, the Flamian lion is displayed in black and basic 'VLM' titles near the front door are in black likewise. Here you can see OO-VLN, the second Fokker F50, on the tarmac at Antwerp-Deurne Airport in late 1993. VLM's international call sign is 'FLANDERS'. *(Author's Collection)*

XP-EXPRESS PARCEL SYSTEM (XP/XPS)
Netherlands

The airline was founded in 1973 as a package delivery courier company with its main centres of activity in Britain, Denmark, Belgium, the Netherlands, Germany, France, Switzerland, Austria and Italy. The company was one of the first to introduce overnight delivery service by means of inter-city parcel flights in Europe between the U.K., the Netherlands and Switzerland in 1984. The home base was Diemen/Amsterdam, although the operational base was Maastricht Airport. All aircraft operated in the beginning were leased. A Fokker F27-600 (PH-FKT) was leased from Kondair, Stansted; a Cessna 414A from Nardi Aero Service SpA and a Piper PA31 from Rijnmond Air Services, BV, Rotterdam. In February 1986, XP-Express Parcel System bought a Fokker F27 from Fokker and three Piper Navajo Chieftains from Rijnmond Air Services. Vendex International held a fifty per cent interest in XPS, KLM Royal Dutch Airlines the remaining fifty per cent. On some of the scheduled night post services XP-Express Parcel System used aircraft operated on behalf of other airlines, like a NFD Swearingen Metro on the Nürnberg-Birmingham route. In January 1987 XP began using the Fokker F27 on the night service Verona-Nürnberg-Maastricht. Another Fokker F27 was leased from Schreiner Airways in July 1987 and operated in full XP colours. Two more Fokker F27s joined the fleet in summer 1988 (ex-Sempati and Luxair). The Piper PA-31 was replaced by leased aircraft from Freeway Air on the Maastricht-Basle service. In May 1989 Rheinland Air Service operated its two Shorts SD360s for XP-Express Parcel System in an all-cargo configuration. At the same time KLM, the owner of XP went into negotiations with TNT Australia concerning a sale of XP. Finally XP-Express Parcel System was sold, fully integrated into TNT and the XP courier services transferred from Cologne to Maastricht. One year later TNT initiated a revival of XP-Express Parcel System. A BAe-146-300 of the Swedish register was painted up in the former XP colours and operated for TNT. Seen here at Nürnberg on 27 August 1987, Fokker F27-400, PH-SFC, is depicted. The aircraft was leased from Schreiner Airways. Originally it had been delivered to the Government of the Ivory Coast in 1971. XPS's ICAO call sign was 'XP PARCEL'. *(W. Kathe)*